Concise Rules of APA Style

American Psychological Association • *Washington, DC*

Copyright © 2005 by the American Psychological Association. All rights reserved. Except as permitted under the United States Copyright Act of 1976, no part of this publication may be reproduced or distributed in any form or by any means, or stored in a database or retrieval system, without the prior written permission of the publisher.

Second Printing June 2005
Third Printing February 2006

Published by
American Psychological Association
750 First Street, NE
Washington, DC 20002
www.apa.org

To order
APA Order Department
P.O. Box 92984
Washington, DC 20090-2984
Tel: (800) 374-2721, Direct: (202) 336-5510
Fax: (202) 336-5502, TDD/TTY: (202) 336-6123
Online: www.apa.org/books/
E-mail: order@apa.org

In the U.K., Europe, Africa, and the Middle East, copies may be ordered from
American Psychological Association
3 Henrietta Street
Covent Garden, London
WC2E 8LU England

Typeset in Sabon and Helvetica by World Composition Services, Sterling, VA

Printer: United Book Press, Baltimore, MD
Cover Designer: Naylor Design, Washington, DC
Production Manager: Jennifer L. Macomber
Production Editor: Dan Brachtesende
Supervisor, Technical Editing and Design: Anne T. Woodworth

Library of Congress Cataloging-in-Publication Data

Concise rules of APA style.
p. cm.
Includes bibliographical references and index.
ISBN 1-59147-252-0
1. Psychology—Authorship—Handbooks, manuals, etc. 2. Social sciences—Authorship—Handbooks, manuals, etc. I. American Psychological Association.

BF76.7.C66 2005
808'.06615—dc22

2004026327

British Library Cataloguing-in-Publication Data
A CIP record is available from the British Library.

Printed in the United States of America
First Edition

Contents

Introduction:
A Pocket Reference for Writers

Welcome to *Concise Rules of APA Style,* the official pocket style guide from the American Psychological Association. Writers who follow these guidelines will express their ideas in a form and a style both accepted by and familiar to a broad, established readership in the social sciences.

Concise Rules of APA Style offers essential writing standards for students, teachers, researchers, and clinicians. These rules have been compiled from the fifth edition of the *Publication Manual of the American Psychological Association* and are drawn from an extensive body of psychological literature. Readers will learn how to avoid the errors in composition and grammar most commonly reported by journal editors; how to choose the appropriate formats for statistics, figures, and tables; how to credit sources and avoid charges of plagiarism; and how to construct a reference list through a wide variety of examples and sources.

Many psychology departments require that student papers, theses, and dissertations be prepared according to APA Style. Of course, where departmental requirements differ from APA Style, the departmental requirements take precedence. Familiarity with both departmental standards and APA Style guidelines will enable students to prepare papers efficiently. Although *Concise Rules of APA Style* is considerably shorter and more compact than the *Publication Manual*, the style guidance it offers is complete. We have selected for our pocket guide those rules of style that are critical for clear communication.

Readers are urged to consult the *Publication Manual* for broad background information about scientific publishing, including guidance on designing research, identifying the parts of a scholarly article, understanding the process of journal publication, and submitting articles for publication. *Concise Rules of APA Style* is offered as a quick-reference supplement to that guide.

We begin in chapter 1 by providing tips to strengthen your scientific writing skills, listing the rules of grammar that have proven to be most challenging to those who submit articles to the APA Journals Program, sharing guidelines to reduce bias in language, and describing the most effective heading structure for organizing your ideas. Chapters 2 and 3 review the mechanics of style for punctuation, spelling, capitalization, abbreviation, and italicization. The preferred use of numbers as well as standards for metrication and statistics are presented in chapter 4. Chapters 5 and 6 provide guidance for the construction and formatting of tables and figures. Instruction on writing and formatting supplemental material is offered in chapter 7. And, finally, complete information on quoting sources and citing references both in text and in the reference list is provided in chapters 8 and 9. For ease of use, we have provided four tools for looking up information: A brief table of contents inside the front cover lists key topics, an expanded table of contents provides detailed entries, an extensive index at the end of the book locates key discussions, and a quick guide to electronic references inside the back cover directs readers to helpful formatting examples. For convenience, we have also included a "Checklist for Manuscript Submission."

Additional guidance can be found at our Web site, http://www.apastyle.org/. This site contains invaluable information on publication ethics, style tips, frequently asked questions, and new resources for writers. Our hope is that the style tools we offer—*Concise Rules of APA Style* in conjunction with the *Publication Manual*—will help readers master the style standards that best foster strong and concise writing in the social sciences.

Gary R. VandenBos, PhD
Publisher, American Psychological Association

1 Concise and Bias-Free Writing

Concise writing is an art and a craft, and instruction in its mastery is beyond the scope of *Concise Rules of APA Style*. This chapter provides some general principles of expository writing, demonstrates how correct grammar can facilitate clear communication, and suggests ways to assess and improve writing style. Grammatical examples should help authors avoid the most common problems that occur in manuscripts submitted to APA journals. The guidelines to reduce bias in language offer suggestions to help authors avoid constructions in their writing that might perpetuate biased assumptions about people.

General Guidance

Orderly Presentation of Ideas

Readers will better understand your ideas if you aim for continuity in words, concepts, and thematic development from the opening statement to the conclusion.

Continuity can be achieved in several ways. For instance, punctuation marks contribute to continuity by showing relationships between ideas. They cue the reader to the pauses, inflections, subordination, and pacing normally heard in speech. Use the full range of punctuation aids available: Neither overuse nor underuse one type of punctuation, such as commas or dashes.

Another way to achieve continuity is through the use of transitional words. These words help maintain the flow of thought, especially when the material is complex or abstract. A pronoun that refers to a noun in the preceding sentence not only serves as a transition but also avoids repetition. Be sure the referent is obvious. Other transition devices are time links (*then, next, after, while, since*), cause–effect links (*therefore, consequently, as a result*), addition links (*in addition, moreover, furthermore, similarly*), and contrast links (*but, conversely, nevertheless, however, although, whereas*).

Smoothness of Expression

Careful use of verb tenses in your writing can help ensure smooth expression. Past tense (e.g., "Smith *showed*") or present perfect tense (e.g., "researchers *have shown*") is appropriate for the literature review and the description of the procedure if the discussion is of past events. Stay within the chosen tense. Use past tense (e.g., "anxiety *decreased* significantly") to describe the results. Use the present tense (e.g., "the results of Experiment 2 *indicate*") to discuss the results and to present the conclusions. By reporting conclusions in the present tense, you allow readers to join you in deliberating the matter at hand. (See Verbs, pp. 8–9, for details on the use of tense.)

Noun strings, meaning several nouns used one after another to modify a final noun, create another form of abruptness. The reader is sometimes forced to stop to determine how the words relate to each other. Skillful hyphenation can clarify the relationships between words, but often the best approach is to untangle the string. For example, consider the following string:

> commonly used investigative expanded issue control question technique

This is dense prose to the reader knowledgeable about studies on lie detection—and gibberish to a reader unfamiliar with such studies. Possible ways to untangle the string are as follows:

- a control-question technique that is commonly used to expand issues in investigations
- an expanded-issue control-question technique that is commonly used in investigations
- a common technique of using control questions to investigate expanded issues
- a common investigative technique of using expanded issues in control questions

One approach to untangling noun strings is to move the last word to the beginning of the string and fill in with verbs and prepositions. For example, "early childhood thought disorder misdiagnosis" might be rearranged to read "misdiagnosis of thought disorders in early childhood."

Economy of Expression

Say only what needs to be said. The author who is frugal with words not only writes a more readable manuscript but also increases the chances that the manuscript will be accepted for publication. The number of printed pages a journal can publish is limited, and editors therefore often request authors to shorten submitted papers. You can tighten long papers by eliminating redundancy, wordiness, jargon, evasiveness, overuse of the passive voice, circumlocution, and clumsy prose. Weed out overly detailed descriptions of apparatus, participants, or procedures (particularly if methods were published elsewhere, in which case you should simply cite the original study); gratuitous embellishments; elaborations of the obvious; and irrelevant observations or asides.

Short words and short sentences are easier to comprehend than are long ones. A long technical term, however, may be more precise than several short words, and technical terms are inseparable from scientific reporting. Yet the technical terminology in a paper should be understood by psychologists throughout the discipline. An article that depends on terminology familiar to only a few specialists does not sufficiently contribute to the literature. The main causes of uneconomical writing are jargon and wordiness.

Jargon. *Jargon* is the continuous use of a technical vocabulary even in places where that vocabulary is not relevant. Jargon is also the substitution of a euphemistic phrase for a familiar term (e.g., *monetarily felt scarcity* for *poverty*), and you should scrupulously avoid using such jargon.

Wordiness. Wordiness is every bit as irritating and uneconomical as jargon and can impede the ready grasp of ideas. Change *based on the fact that* to *because*, *at the present time* to *now*, and *for the purpose of* to simply *for* or *to*. Use *this study* instead of *the present study* when the context is clear. Unconstrained wordiness lapses into embellishment and flowery writing, which are inappropriate in scientific style.

Redundancy. Writers often become redundant in an effort to be emphatic. Use no more words than are necessary to convey your meaning. In the following examples, the italicized words are redundant and should be omitted:

They were *both* alike
a total of 68 participants
Four *different* groups saw
instructions, which were *exactly* the same as those used
absolutely essential
has been *previously* found
small *in size*
one and the same
in *close* proximity
completely unanimous
just exactly
very close to significance
period of time
summarize *briefly*
the reason is *because*

Precision and Clarity

Word Choice. Make certain that every word means exactly what you intend it to mean. In informal style, for example, *feel* broadly substitutes for *think* or *believe*, but in scientific style such latitude is not acceptable.

Colloquial Expressions. Likewise, avoid colloquial expressions (e.g., *write up* for *report*), which diffuse meaning. Approximations of quantity (e.g., *quite a large part, practically all,* or *very few*) are interpreted differently by different readers or in different contexts. Approximations weaken statements, especially those describing empirical observations.

Pronouns. Pronouns confuse readers unless the referent for each pronoun is obvious; readers should not have to search previous text to determine the meaning of the term. Simple pronouns are the most troublesome, especially *this, that, these,* and *those* when they refer to a previous sentence. Eliminate ambiguity by writing, for example, *this test, that trial, these participants,* and *those reports*. (See also Pronouns, pp. 11–13.)

Comparisons. Ambiguous or illogical comparisons result from omission of key verbs or from nonparallel structure. Consider, for example, "Ten-year-olds were more likely to play with age peers than 8-year-olds." Does this sentence mean that 10-year-olds were more likely than 8-year-olds to play with age peers? Or does it mean that 10-year-olds were more likely to play with age peers and less likely to play with 8-year-olds? An illogical comparison occurs when parallelism is overlooked for the sake of brevity, as in "Her salary was lower than a convenience store clerk." Thoughtful attention to good sentence structure and word choice reduces the chance of this kind of ambiguity.

Attribution. Inappropriately or illogically attributing action in an effort to be objective can be misleading. Examples of undesirable attribution include use of the third person, anthropomorphism, and use of the editorial *we*.

- **third person:** Writing "The experimenters instructed the participants" when "the experimenters" refers to yourself is ambiguous and may give the impression that you did not take part in your own study. Instead, use a personal pronoun: "We instructed the participants."

- **anthropomorphism:** In addition, do not attribute human characteristics to animals or to inanimate sources.

Anthropomorphism:

Ancestral horses probably traveled as wild horses do today, either in bands of bachelor males or in harems of mares headed by a single stallion.

Solution:

Ancestral horses probably traveled as wild horses do today, either in bands of males or in groups of several mares and a stallion.

Anthropomorphism:

The community program was persuaded to allow five of the observers to become tutors.

Solution:

The staff for the community program was persuaded to allow five of the observers to become tutors.

- **editorial *we*:** For clarity, restrict your use of *we* to refer only to yourself and your coauthors (use *I* if you are the sole author of the paper). Broader uses of *we* leave your readers to determine to whom you are referring; instead, substitute an appropriate noun or clarify your usage:

Poor:

We usually classify birdsong on the basis of frequency and temporal structure of the elements.

Better:

Researchers usually classify birdsong on the basis of frequency and temporal structure of the elements.

Grammar

Incorrect grammar and careless construction of sentences distract the reader, introduce ambiguity, and generally obstruct communication. The examples in this chapter represent the kinds of problems of grammar and usage that occur frequently in manuscripts submitted to APA journals. These examples should help authors steer clear of the most common errors.

Verbs

Verbs are vigorous, direct communicators. Use the active rather than the passive voice, and select tense and mood carefully.

Prefer the active voice.

Poor:

The survey was conducted in a controlled setting.

Better:

We conducted the survey in a controlled setting.

The passive voice is acceptable in expository writing and when you want to focus on the object or recipient of an action rather than on the actor. For example, "The speakers were attached to either side of the chair" emphasizes the placement of speakers, not who placed them—placement may be the appropriate focus in the Method section of a journal article. Use the past tense to express an action or a condition that occurred at a specific, definite time in the past, as when discussing another researcher's work and when reporting your results.

Incorrect:

Sanchez (2000) presents the same results.

Correct:

Sanchez (2000) presented the same results.

Use the present perfect tense to express a past action or condition that did not occur at a specific, definite time or to describe an action beginning in the past and continuing to the present.

Incorrect:

Since that time, investigators from several studies used this method.

Correct:

Since that time, investigators from several studies have used this method.

Use the subjunctive mood to describe only conditions that are contrary to fact or improbable; do not use the subjunctive to describe simple conditions or contingencies.

Incorrect:

If the experiment was not designed this way, the participants' performances would suffer.

Correct:

If the experiment were not designed this way, the participants' performances would suffer.

Agreement of Subject and Verb

A verb must agree in number (i.e., singular or plural) with its subject, regardless of intervening phrases that begin with such words as *together with*, *including*, *plus*, and *as well as*.

Incorrect:

The percentage of correct responses as well as the speed of the responses increase with practice.

Correct:

The percentage of correct responses as well as the speed of the responses increases with practice.

The plural form of some nouns of foreign origin, particularly those that end in the letter *a,* may appear to be singular and can cause authors to select a verb that does not agree in number with the noun:

Incorrect:

The data indicates that Terrence was correct.

Correct:

The data indicate that Terrence was correct.

Incorrect:

The phenomena occurs every 100 years.

Correct:

The phenomena occur every 100 years.

Collective nouns (e.g., *series, set, faculty,* or *pair*) can refer either to several individuals or to a single unit. If the action of the verb is on the group as a whole, treat the noun as a singular noun. If the action of the verb is on members of the group as individuals, treat the noun as a plural noun. The context (i.e., your emphasis) determines whether the action is on the group or on individuals.

Singular in context:

The number of people in the state is growing.

A pair of animals was in each cage.

Plural in context:

A number of people are watching.

A pair of animals were then yoked.

The pronoun *none* can also be singular or plural. When the noun that follows it is singular, use a singular verb; when the noun is plural, use a plural verb. If you mean "not one," use *not one* instead of *none* and use a singular verb.

Singular in context:

None of the information was correct.

Plural in context:

None of the children were finished in the time allotted.

but

Not one of the children was finished in the time allotted.

When the subject is composed of a singular and a plural noun joined by *or* or *nor*, the verb agrees with the noun that is closer.

Incorrect:

Neither the participants nor the confederate were in the room.

Correct:

Neither the participants nor the confederate was in the room.

or

Neither the confederate nor the participants were in the room.

If the number of the subject changes, retain the verb in each clause.

Incorrect:

The positions in the sequence were changed, and the test rerun.

Correct:

The positions in the sequence were changed, and the test was rerun.

Pronouns

Pronouns replace nouns. Each pronoun should refer clearly to its antecedent and should agree with the antecedent in number and gender.

A pronoun must agree in number (i.e., singular or plural) with the noun it replaces.

Incorrect:

Neither the highest scorer nor the lowest scorer in the group had any doubt about their competence.

Correct:

Neither the highest scorer nor the lowest scorer in the group had any doubt about his or her competence.

A pronoun must agree in gender (i.e., masculine, feminine, or neuter) with the noun it replaces. This rule extends to relative pronouns (pronouns that link subordinate clauses to nouns). Use *who* for people; use *that* or *which* for animals and for things.

Incorrect:

The rats who completed the task successfully were rewarded.

Correct:

The rats that completed the task successfully were rewarded.

Use neuter pronouns to refer to animals (e.g., "the dog . . . it") unless the animals have been named:

The chimps were tested daily. . . . Sheba was tested unrestrained in an open testing area, which was her usual context for training and testing.

Pronouns can be subjects or objects of verbs or prepositions. Use *who* as the subject of a verb and *whom* as the object of a verb or a preposition. You can determine whether a relative pronoun is the subject or object of a verb by turning the subordinate clause around and substituting a personal pronoun. If you can substitute *he* or *she*, *who* is correct; if you can substitute *him* or *her*, *whom* is the correct pronoun.

Incorrect:

Name the participant whom you found achieved scores above the median. [You found *him* or *her* achieved scores above the median.]

Correct:

Name the participant who you found achieved scores above the median. [You found *he* or *she* achieved scores above the median.]

Incorrect:

The participant who I identified as the youngest dropped out. [I identified *he* or *she* as the youngest.]

Correct:

The participant whom I identified as the youngest dropped out. [I identified *him* or *her* as the youngest.

In a phrase consisting of a pronoun or noun plus a present participle (e.g., *running, flying*) that is used as an object of a preposition, the participle can be either a noun or a modifier of a noun, depending on the intended meaning. When you use a participle as a noun, make the other pronoun or noun possessive.

Incorrect:

We had nothing to do with them being the winners.

Correct:

We had nothing to do with their being the winners.

Incorrect:

The significance is questionable because of 1 participant performing at incredible speed.

Correct:

The significance is questionable because of 1 participant's performing at incredible speed. [The significance is questionable because of the performance, not because of the participant.]

but

We spoke to the person sitting at the table. [The person, not the sitting, is the object of the preposition.]

Misplaced and Dangling Modifiers and Use of Adverbs

An adjective or an adverb, whether a single word or a phrase, must clearly refer to the word it modifies.

Misplaced modifiers, because of their placement in a sentence, ambiguously or illogically modify a word. You can eliminate these by placing an adjective or an adverb as close as possible to the word it modifies.

Unclear:

The investigator tested the participants using this procedure. [The sentence is unclear about whether the investigator or the participants used this procedure.]

Clear:

Using this procedure, the investigator tested the participants.

Clear:

The investigator tested the participants who were using the procedure.

Incorrect:

Based on this assumption, we developed a model. . . . [This construction says, "we are based on an assumption."]

Correct:

On the basis of this assumption, we developed a model. . . .

Based on this assumption, the model. . . .

Many writers have trouble with the word *only*. Place *only* next to the word or phrase it modifies.

Incorrect:

These data only provide a partial answer.

Correct:

These data provide only a partial answer.

Dangling modifiers have no referent in the sentence. Many of these result from the use of passive voice. By writing in the active voice, you can avoid many dangling modifiers.

Incorrect:

The participants were tested using this procedure.

Correct:

Using this procedure, I tested the participants. [I, not the participants, used the procedure.]

Incorrect:

To test this hypothesis, the participants were divided into two groups.

Correct:

To test this hypothesis, we divided the participants into two groups. [We, not the participants, tested the hypothesis.]

Adverbs can be used as introductory or transitional words. Adverbs modify verbs, adjectives, and other adverbs and express manner or quality. Some adverbs, however—such as *fortunately, similarly, certainly, consequently, conversely,* and *regrettably*—can also be used as introductory or transitional words as long as the sense is confined to, for example, "it is fortunate that" or "in a similar manner." Use adverbs judiciously as introductory or transitional words. Ask yourself whether the introduction or transition is needed and whether the adverb is being used correctly.

Some of the more common introductory adverbial phrases are *importantly, more importantly,* and *interestingly*. Although *importantly* is used widely, whether its adverbial usage is proper is debatable. Both *importantly* and *interestingly* can often be recast to enhance the message of a sentence or simply be omitted without a loss of meaning.

Problematic:

> More importantly, the total amount of available long-term memory activation, and not the rate of spreading activation, drives the rate and probability of retrieval.

Preferred:

> More important, the total amount of available long-term memory activation, and not the rate of spreading activation, drives the rate and probability of retrieval.

Correct adverbial usage:

> Expressive behavior and autonomic nervous system activity also have figured importantly. . . .

Problematic:

> Interestingly, the total amount of available long-term memory activation, and not the rate of spreading activation, drives the rate and probability of retrieval.

Preferred:

> We were surprised to learn that the total. . . .
>
> We find it interesting that the total. . . .
>
> An interesting finding was that. . . .

Relative Pronouns and Subordinate Conjunctions

Relative pronouns (*who, whom, that, which*) and subordinate conjunctions (e.g., *since, while, although*) introduce an element that is subordinate to the main clause of the sentence and reflect the relationship of the subordinate element to the main clause. Therefore, select these pronouns and conjunctions with care.

Relative Pronouns

***That* versus *which*.** *That* clauses (called *restrictive*) are essential to the meaning of the sentence:

The animals that performed well in the first experiment were used in the second experiment.

Which clauses can merely add further information (nonrestrictive) or can be essential to the meaning (restrictive) of the sentence. APA prefers to reserve *which* for nonrestrictive clauses and use *that* in restrictive clauses.

Nonrestrictive:

The animals, which performed well in the first experiment, were not proficient in the second experiment. [The second experiment was more difficult for all of the animals.]

Restrictive:

The animals which performed well in the first experiment were not proficient in the second experiment. [Only those animals that performed well in the first experiment were not proficient in the second; prefer *that*.]

Consistent use of *that* for restrictive clauses and *which* for nonrestrictive clauses, which are set off with commas, will help make your writing clear and precise.

Subordinate Conjunctions

***While* and *since*.** Some style authorities accept the use of *while* and *since* when they do not refer strictly to time; however, words like these, with more than one meaning, can cause confusion. Because precision and clarity are the standards in scientific writing, restricting your use of *while* and *since* to their temporal meanings is helpful.

***While* versus *although*.** Use *while* to link events occurring simultaneously; use *although*, *whereas*, *and*, or *but* in place of *while*.

Imprecise:

Bragg (1965) found that participants performed well, while Bohr (1969) found that participants did poorly.

Precise:

Bragg (1965) found that participants performed well, whereas Bohr (1969) found that participants did poorly.

Imprecise:

While these findings are unusual, they are not unique.

Precise:

Although these findings are unusual, they are not unique.

Since* versus *because. *Since* is more precise when it is used to refer only to time (to mean "after that"); otherwise, replace with *because.*

Imprecise:

Data for 2 participants were incomplete since these participants did not report for follow up testing.

Precise:

Data for 2 participants were incomplete because these participants did not report for follow-up testing.

Parallel Construction

To enhance the reader's understanding, present parallel ideas in parallel or coordinate form. Make certain that all elements of the parallelism are present before and after the coordinating conjunction (i.e., *and, but, or, nor*).

Incorrect:

The results show that such changes could be made without affecting error rate and latencies continued to decrease over time.

Correct:

The results show that such changes could be made without affecting error rate and that latencies continued to decrease over time.

With coordinating conjunctions used in pairs (*between . . . and, both . . . and, neither . . . nor, either . . . or, not only . . . but also*), place the first conjunction immediately before the first part of the parallelism.

Between* and *and

Incorrect:

We recorded the difference between the performance of subjects that completed the first task and the second task.

Correct:

We recorded the difference between the performance of subjects that completed the first task and the performance of those that completed the second task. [The difference is between the subjects' performances, not between the performance and the task.]

Incorrect:

between 2.5–4.0 years of age

Correct:

between 2.5 and 4.0 years of age

Both* and *and

Incorrect:

The names were both difficult to pronounce and spell.

Correct:

The names were difficult both to pronounce and to spell.

Never use *both* with *as well as*: The resulting construction is redundant.

Incorrect:

The names were difficult both to pronounce as well as to spell.

Correct:

The names were difficult to pronounce as well as to spell.

Neither* and *nor* and *either* and *or

Incorrect:

Neither the responses to the auditory stimuli nor to the tactile stimuli were repeated.

Correct:

Neither the responses to the auditory stimuli nor the responses to the tactile stimuli were repeated.

Incorrect:

The respondents either gave the worst answer or the best answer.

Correct:

The respondents either gave the worst answer or gave the best answer. [The respondents gave either the worst answer or the best answer.]

Not only* and *but (also)

Incorrect:

It is not only surprising that pencil-and-paper scores predicted this result but that all other predictors were less accurate.

Correct:

It is surprising not only that pencil-and-paper scores predicted this result but also that all other predictors were less accurate.

Elements in a series should also be parallel in form.

Incorrect:

The participants were told to make themselves comfortable, to read the instructions, and that they should ask about anything they did not understand.

Correct:

The participants were told to make themselves comfortable, to read the instructions, and to ask about anything they did not understand.

Linguistic Devices

Devices that attract attention to words, sounds, or other embellishments instead of to ideas are inappropriate in scientific writing. Avoid heavy alliteration, rhyming, poetic expressions, and clichés. Use metaphors sparingly; although they can help simplify complicated ideas, metaphors can be distracting. Avoid mixed metaphors (e.g., *a theory representing one branch of a growing body of evidence*) and words with surplus or unintended meaning (e.g., *cop* for *police officer*), which may distract if not actually mislead the reader. Use figurative expressions with restraint and colorful expressions with care; these expressions can sound strained or forced.

Reducing Bias in Language

As a publisher, APA accepts authors' word choices unless those choices are inaccurate, unclear, or ungrammatical. As an organization, APA is committed both to science and to the fair treatment of individuals and groups, and this policy requires authors of APA publications to avoid perpetuating biased assumptions about people in their writing. Constructions that might imply bias against persons on the basis of gender, sexual orientation, racial or ethnic group, disability, or age should be avoided. Scientific writing should be free of implied or irrelevant evaluation of the group or groups being studied.

Long-standing cultural practice can exert a powerful influence over even the most conscientious author. Just as you have learned to check what you write for spelling, grammar, and wordiness, practice reading over your work for bias.

What follows is a set of guidelines, followed in turn by discussions of specific issues that affect particular groups. These are not rigid rules. You may find that some attempts to follow the guidelines result in wordiness or clumsy prose. As always, good judgment is required.

Guideline 1: Describe at the Appropriate Level of Specificity

Precision is a necessity in scientific writing; when you refer to a person or persons, choose words that are accurate, clear, and free from bias. The appropriate degree of specificity depends on the research question and the present state of knowledge in the field of study. When in doubt, it is better to be more specific rather than less, because it is easier to aggregate published data than to disaggregate them. For example, using *man* to refer to all people is simply not as accurate as using *people* or the phrase *men and women*. When describing age groups, it is better to give a specific age range ("ages 65–83") instead of a broad category ("over 65"; see Schaie, 1993).

Gender is cultural and is the term to use when referring to men and women as social groups. *Sex* is biological; use it when the biological distinction is predominant. Note that the word *sex* can be confused with *sexual behavior. Gender* helps keep meaning unambiguous, as in the following example: "In accounting for attitudes toward the bill, sexual orientation rather than gender accounted for most of the variance. Most gay men and lesbians were for the proposal; most heterosexual men and women were against it."

Part of writing without bias is recognizing that differences should be mentioned only when relevant. Marital status, sexual orientation, racial and ethnic identity, or the fact that a person has a disability should not be mentioned gratuitously.

Guideline 2: Be Sensitive to Labels

Respect people's preferences; call people what they prefer to be called (Maggio, 1991). Accept that preferences will change with time and that individuals within groups often disagree about the designations they prefer (see Raspberry, 1989). Make an effort to determine what is appropriate for your situation; you may need to ask your participants which designations they prefer, particularly when preferred designations are being debated within groups.

Avoid labeling people when possible. A common occurrence in scientific writing is that participants in a study tend to lose their individuality; they are broadly categorized as objects (noun forms such as *the gays* and *the elderly*) or, particularly in descriptions of people with disabilities, are equated with their conditions—*the amnesiacs, the depressives, the schizophrenics, the LDs*, for example. One solution is to use adjectival forms (e.g., "gay *men*," "elderly *people*," "amnesic *patients*"). Another is to "put the person first," followed by a descriptive phrase (e.g., "people diagnosed with schizophrenia"). Note that the latter solution currently is preferred when describing people with disabilities.

When you need to mention several groups in a sentence or paragraph, such as when reporting results, do your best to balance sensitivity, clarity, and parsimony. For example, it may be cumbersome to repeat phrases such as "person with ____." If you provide operational definitions of groups early in your paper (e.g., "Participants scoring a minimum of X on the X scale constituted the high verbal group, and those scoring below X constituted the low verbal group"), it is scientifically informative and concise to describe participants thereafter in terms of the measures used to classify them (e.g., " . . . was significant: high verbal group, $p < .05$"), *provided the terms are inoffensive*. A label should not be used in any form that is perceived as pejorative; if such a perception is possible, you need to find more neutral terms.

Bias may be promoted when the writer uses one group (usually the writer's own group) as the standard against which others are judged. In some contexts, the term *culturally deprived* may imply that one culture is the universally accepted standard. The unparallel nouns in the phrase *man and wife* may inappropriately prompt the reader to evaluate the roles of the individuals (i.e., the woman is defined only in terms of her relationship to the man) and the motives of the author. Usage of *normal* may prompt the reader to make the comparison of *abnormal*, thus stigmatizing individuals with differences. For example, contrasting lesbians with "the general public" or with "normal women" portrays lesbians as marginal to society. More appropriate comparison groups might be "heterosexual women," "heterosexual women and men," or "gay men."

Guideline 3: Acknowledge Participation

Write about the people in your study in a way that acknowledges their participation. Replace the impersonal term *subjects* with a more descriptive term when appropriate—*participants, individuals, college students, children,* or *respondents,* for example. *Subjects* and *sample* are appropriate when discussing statistics, and *subjects* may also be appropriate when there has been no direct consent by the individual involved in the study (e.g., infants or some individuals with severe brain damage or dementia). The passive voice suggests individuals are *acted on* instead of being actors ("the students *completed* the survey" is preferable to "the students *were given* the survey" or "the survey *was administered* to the students"). Similarly, consider avoiding terms such as *patient management* and *patient placement* when appropriate. In most cases, it is treatment, not patients, that is managed; some alternatives are "coordination of care," "supportive services," and "assistance." *Failed,* as in "8 participants failed to complete the Rorschach and the MMPI," can imply a personal shortcoming instead of a research result; *did not* is a more neutral choice (Knatterud, 1991).

Gender

Avoid ambiguity in sex identity or sex role by choosing nouns, pronouns, and adjectives that specifically describe your participants. Sexist bias can occur when pronouns are used carelessly, as when the masculine pronoun *he* is used to refer to both sexes or when the masculine or feminine pronoun is used exclusively to define roles by sex (e.g., "the nurse . . . *she*"). The use of *man* as a generic noun or as an ending for an occupational title (e.g., *policeman*) can be ambiguous and may imply incorrectly that all persons in the group are male. Be clear about whether you mean one sex or both sexes.

There are many alternatives to the generic *he*, including rephrasing (e.g., "When an individual conducts this kind of self-appraisal, *that person* is much stronger" or "This kind of self-appraisal makes an individual much stronger"), using plural nouns or plural pronouns (e.g., "Therapists who are too much like *their* clients can lose *their* objectivity"), and replacing the pronoun with an article (e.g., "A researcher must apply for *the* grant by September 1"). Replacing *he* with *he or she* or *she or he* should be done sparingly because the repetition can become tiresome. Combination forms such as *he/she* or *(s)he* are awkward and distracting. Alternating between *he* and *she* also may be distracting and is not ideal.

Sexual Orientation

Sexual orientation is not the same as *sexual preference.* In keeping with Guideline 2, *sexual orientation* currently is the preferred term and is to be used unless the implication of choice is intentional.

The terms *lesbians* and *gay men* are preferable to *homosexual* when referring to specific groups. *Lesbian* and *gay* refer primarily to identities and to the culture and communities that have developed among people who share those identities. Furthermore, *homosexuality* has been associated in the past with negative stereotypes. Also, the term *homosexual* is ambiguous because some believe it refers only to men. *Gay* can be interpreted broadly, to include men and women, or more narrowly, to include only men. Therefore, if the meaning is not clear in the context of your usage, specify gender when using this term (e.g., *gay men*). The clearest way to refer inclusively to people whose orientation is not heterosexual is to write *lesbians, gay men, and bisexual women or men*—although somewhat long, the phrase is accurate.

Sexual behavior should be distinguished from sexual orientation; some men and women engage in sexual activities with others of their own sex but do not consider themselves to be gay or lesbian. In contrast, the terms *heterosexual* and *bisexual* currently are used to describe both identity and behavior; adjectives are preferred to nouns. *Same-gender, male–male, female–female,* and *male–female sexual behavior* are appropriate terms for specific instances of sexual behavior in which people engage, regardless of their sexual orientation (e.g., a married heterosexual man who once had a same-gender sexual encounter).

Racial and Ethnic Identity

Preferences for terms referring to racial and ethnic groups change often. One reason for this is simply personal preference; preferred designations are as varied as the people they name. Another reason is that over time, designations can become dated and sometimes negative (see Raspberry, 1989). Some people of African ancestry prefer *Black* and others prefer *African American*; both terms currently are acceptable. On the other hand, *Negro* and *Afro-American* have become dated; therefore, usage generally is inappropriate.

Racial and ethnic groups are designated by proper nouns and are capitalized. Therefore, use *Black* and *White* instead of *black* and *white* (colors to refer to other human groups currently are considered pejorative and should not be used). For modifiers, do not use hyphens in multiword names, even if the names act as unit modifiers (e.g., *Asian American* participants).

Depending on where a person is from, he or she may prefer to be called *Hispanic, Latino, Chicano,* or some other designation; *Hispanic* is not necessarily an all-encompassing term, and authors should consult with their participants. In general, naming a nation or region of origin is generally helpful (e.g., *Cuban* or *Central American* is more specific than *Hispanic*).

American Indian and *Native American* are both accepted terms for referring to indigenous peoples of North America, although *Native Americans* is a broader designation because the U.S. government includes Hawaiians and Samoans in this category. There are close to 450 Native groups, and authors are encouraged to name the participants' specific groups.

The term *Asian* or *Asian American* is preferred to the older term *Oriental*. It is generally useful to specify the name of the Asian subgroup: Chinese, Vietnamese, Korean, Pakistani, and so on.

Disabilities

The guiding principle for "nonhandicapping" language is to maintain the integrity of individuals as human beings. Avoid language that equates persons with their condition (e.g., *neurotics*, *the disabled*); that has superfluous, negative overtones (e.g., stroke *victim*); or that is regarded as a slur (e.g., *cripple*).

Use *disability* to refer to an attribute of a person and *handicap* to refer to the source of limitations, which may include attitudinal, legal, and architectural barriers as well as the disability itself (e.g., steps and curbs handicap people who require the use of a ramp). *Challenged* and *special* are often considered euphemistic and should be used only if the people in your study prefer those terms (Boston, 1992). As a general rule, "person with ____," "person living with ____," and "person who has ____" are neutral and preferred forms of description.

Age

Age should be defined in the description of participants in the Method section of a journal article. Be specific in providing age ranges; avoid open-ended definitions such as "under 18" or "over 65" (Schaie, 1993). *Boy* and *girl* are correct terms for referring to people of high school age and younger. *Young man* and *young woman* and *male adolescent* and *female adolescent* may be used as appropriate. For persons 18 and older (or of college age and older), use *men* and *women*. *Elderly* is not acceptable as a noun and is considered pejorative by some as an adjective. *Older person* is preferred. Age groups may also be described with adjectives; gerontologists may prefer to use combination terms for older age groups (*young-old, old-old, very old,* and *oldest old*), which should be used only as adjectives. *Dementia* is preferred to *senility*; *senile dementia of the Alzheimer's type* is an accepted term.

Organizing Ideas

Organizing a Manuscript With Headings

Levels of heading establish through format or appearance the hierarchy of sections to orient the reader. All topics of equal importance have the same level of heading throughout a manuscript. For example, in a multi-experiment paper, the headings for the Method and Results sections in Experiment 1 should be the same level as the headings for the Method and Results sections in Experiment 2.

In manuscripts submitted to APA journals, headings function as an outline to reveal a manuscript's organization. Avoid having only one subsection heading and subsection within a section, just as you would avoid in an outline. Use at least two subsection headings within any given section, or use none (e.g., in an outline, you could divide a section numbered I into a minimum of A and B sections; just an A section could not stand alone).

Regardless of the number of levels of subheading within a section, the heading structure for all sections follows the same top-down progression. Each section starts with the highest level of heading, even if one section may have fewer levels of subheading than another section. For example, the Method and Results sections of a paper may each have two levels of subheading, and the Discussion section may have only one level of subheading. There would then be three levels of heading for the paper overall: the section headings (Method, Results, and Discussion) and the two levels of subheading, as follows:

Method

Sample and Procedures

Measures

Perceived control.

Behavior and emotion.

Results

Analyses

Descriptive statistics.

Intraconstruct correlations.

Interconstruct correlations.

Unique Effects of Perceived Control on Behavior and Emotion

Motivational Profiles

Discussion

Limitations of the Study

Implications for Intervention

Conclusions

APA's heading style consists of five possible formatting arrangements, according to the number of levels of subordination. Each heading level is numbered (Level 1, Level 2, etc.), but the specific levels used are not necessarily consecutive. Follow the guidelines in the next section to select the proper heading style according to the levels of subordination within your paper.

If your paper has a complex organization, or if you find it difficult to follow APA heading style, you may submit an outline with your accepted manuscript for the copy editor to follow to ensure that your paper is organized as you envision.

The introduction to a manuscript does not carry a heading labeling it the introduction (the first part of a manuscript is assumed to be the introduction). Therefore if the introduction contains headings, the first heading and later equivalent headings within the section are assigned the highest level of heading (Level 1 for all but five-level papers).

Levels of Heading

The five levels of headings in APA journals are formatted as follows:

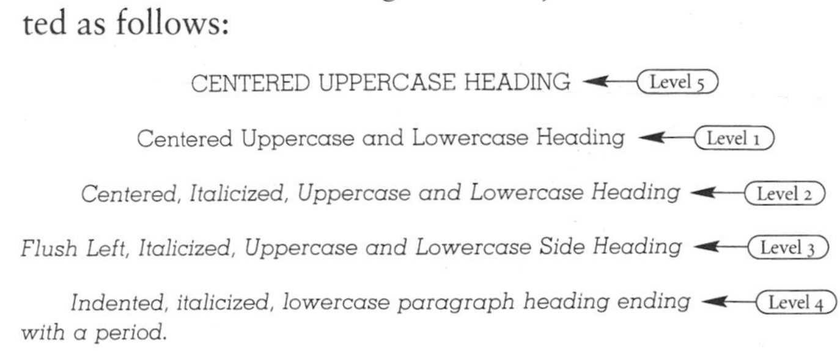

CENTERED UPPERCASE HEADING
Level 5
Centered Uppercase and Lowercase Heading
Level 1
Centered, Italicized, Uppercase and Lowercase Heading
Level 2
Flush Left, Italicized, Uppercase and Lowercase Side Heading
Level 3
Indented, italicized, lowercase paragraph heading ending with a period.
Level 4

The headings for an article using all five levels of heading would be formatted as follows:

EXPERIMENT 1: AN INTERVIEW VALIDATION STUDY

External Validation

Method

Participants

Sleep-deprived group.

Selecting the Levels of Heading

Find the section of your paper that breaks into the finest level of subordinate categories. Then use the guidelines that follow to determine the level, position, and arrangement of headings.

One Level. For a short article, one level of heading may be sufficient. In such cases, use only centered uppercase and lowercase headings (Level 1).

Two Levels. For many articles in APA journals, two levels of heading meet the requirements. Use Level 1 and Level 3 headings:

If the material subordinate to the Level 1 headings is short or if many Level 3 headings are necessary, indented, italicized lowercase paragraph headings (Level 4) may be more appropriate than Level 3 headings. (A Level 4 heading should apply to all text between it and the next heading, regardless of the heading level of the next heading.)

Three Levels. For some articles, three levels of heading are needed. Use Level 1, Level 3, and Level 4 headings.

In a *single-experiment study*, these three levels of heading may look like this:

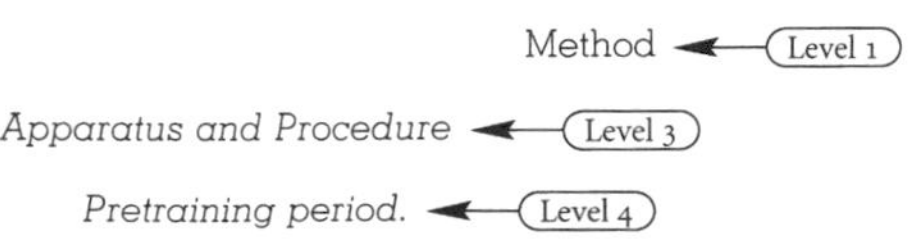

In a *multiexperiment study*, these three levels of heading may look like this:

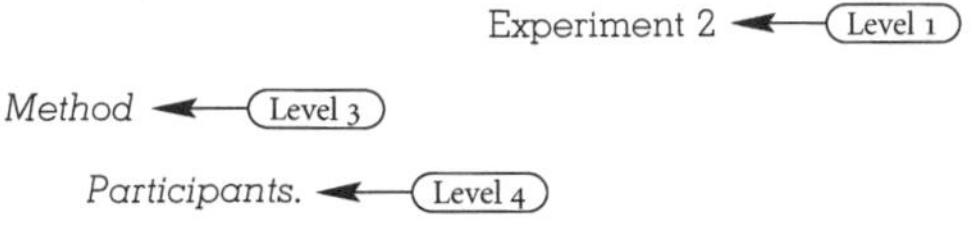

Four Levels. For many articles, particularly multiexperiment studies, monographs, and lengthy literature reviews, four levels of heading are needed. Use heading Levels 1 through 4:

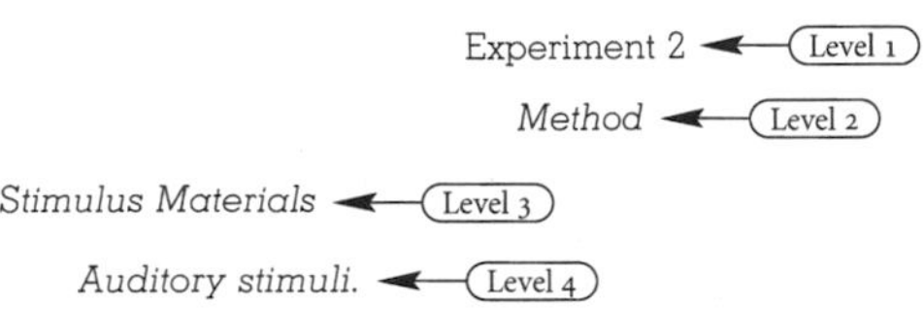

Five Levels. Occasionally, an article requires five levels of heading. In such cases, subordinate all four levels above by introducing a Level 5 heading—a centered uppercase heading—above the other four (as shown previously in Levels of Heading, p. 27).

2 Punctuation, Spelling, and Capitalization

Editorial style concerns uniform use of punctuation and abbreviations, construction of tables, selection of headings, and citation of references, as well as many other elements that are part of every manuscript. An author writing for a publication is asked to follow the style rules established by the publisher to avoid inconsistencies among journal articles or book chapters.

This chapter describes the style for APA journals regarding punctuation, spelling, and capitalization. It omits general rules explained in widely available style books and examples of usage with little relevance to APA journals. Among the most helpful general guides to editorial style are *Words into Type* (Skillin & Gay, 1974) and the *Chicago Manual of Style* (University of Chicago Press, 2003), both of which were used in developing this chapter as well as chapters 3 through 7. Style manuals agree more often than they disagree; where they disagree, the *Publication Manual*, because it is based on the special requirements of psychology, takes precedence for APA publications.

Punctuation

Punctuation establishes the cadence of a sentence, telling the reader where to pause (comma, semicolon, and colon), stop (period and question mark), or take a detour (dash, parentheses, and brackets; Nurnberg, 1972). Punctuation of a sentence usually denotes a pause in thought; different kinds of punctuation indicate different kinds and lengths of pauses.

Period

Use a period to end a complete sentence. For other uses of periods, see the following sections: Abbreviations (pp. 51–58), Quotations (pp. 125–131), Numbers (pp. 59–65), Reference Citations in Text (pp. 131–137), and Reference List (pp. 137–149); see also chapter 9.

Comma

Use a comma

- between elements (including before *and* and *or*) in a series of three or more items. (See Seriation, pp. 59–60, for use of commas in numbered or lettered series.)

  the height, width, or depth

  in a study by Stacy, Newcomb, and Bentler (1991)

- to set off a nonessential or nonrestrictive clause, that is, a clause that embellishes a sentence but if removed would leave the grammatical structure and meaning of the sentence intact.

  Switch A, which was on a panel, controlled the recording device.

  Significant differences were found for both ratings of controllability by self, $F(3, 132) = 19.58$, $p \leq .01$, est $\eta^2 = .31$, and ratings of controllability by others, $F(3, 96) = 3.21$, $p = .03$, est $\eta^2 = .09$.

- to separate two independent clauses joined by a conjunction.

  Cedar shavings covered the floor, and paper was available for shredding and nest building.

- to set off the year in exact dates.

  April 18, 1992, was the correct date.

but

  April 1992 was the correct month.

- to set off the year in parenthetical reference citations.

  (Patrick, 1993)

  (Kelsey, 1993, discovered . . .)

- to separate groups of three digits in most numbers of 1,000 or more (see Commas in Numbers, p. 65, for exceptions).

Do not use a comma

- before an essential or restrictive clause, that is, a clause that limits or defines the material it modifies. Removal of such a clause from a sentence would alter the intended meaning.

The switch that stops the recording device also controls the light.

- between the two parts of a compound predicate.

  The results contradicted Smith's hypothesis and indicated that the effect was nonsignificant.

- to separate parts of measurement.

  8 years 2 months 3 min 40 s

Semicolon

Use a semicolon

- to separate two independent clauses that are not joined by a conjunction.

  The participants in the first study were paid; those in the second were unpaid.

- to separate elements in a series that already contain commas. (See Seriation, p. 59, for the use of semicolons in numbered or lettered series.)

  The color order was red, yellow, blue; blue, yellow, red; or yellow, red, blue.

  (Davis & Hueter, 1994; Pettigrew, 1993)

  main effects of age, $F(1, 76) = 7.86$, $p < .01$, $d = .09$ ($MSE = .019$); condition, $F(1, 76) = 4.11$, $p = .05$, $d = .06$; and the Age × Condition interaction, $F(1, 76) = 4.96$, $p = .03$, $d = .07$

Colon

Use a colon

- between a grammatically complete introductory clause (one that could stand as a sentence) and a final phrase or clause that illustrates, extends, or amplifies the preceding thought. If the clause following the colon is a complete sentence, it begins with a capital letter.

  For example, Freud (1930/1961) wrote of two urges: an urge toward union with others and an egoistic urge toward happiness.

  They have agreed on the outcome: Informed participants perform better than do uninformed participants.

- in ratios and proportions.

  The proportion (salt:water) was 1:8.

- in references between place of publication and publisher.

  New York: Wiley. St. Louis, MO: Mosby.

Do not use a colon

- after an introduction that is not a complete sentence.

  The formula is $r_i = e + a$

Dash

Use the dash to indicate only a sudden interruption in the continuity of a sentence. Overuse weakens the flow of material. (See also Major Words in Titles and Headings, pp. 43–44, for capitalization following dashes in titles.)

These 2 participants—1 from the first group, 1 from the second—were tested separately.

Quotation Marks

Observe the following guidelines for uses of double quotation marks other than in material quoted directly from a source. (See Quotations, pp. 125–127, for a discussion of double and single quotation marks in quoted material.)

Use double quotation marks

- to introduce a word or phrase used as an ironic comment, as slang, or as an invented or coined expression. Use quotation marks the first time the word or phrase is used; thereafter, do not use quotation marks.

  considered "normal" behavior

  the "good-outcome" variable . . . the good-outcome variable [no quotation marks after the initial usage]

- to set off the title of an article or chapter in a periodical or book when the title is mentioned in text. (Titles in the reference list are not enclosed in quotation marks; see Title of Article or Chapter, p. 145.)

  Riger's (1992) article, "Epistemological Debates, Feminist Voices: Science, Social Values, and the Study of Women"

- to reproduce material from a test item or verbatim instructions to participants.

  The first fill-in item was "could be expected to ________."

  If instructions are long, set them off from text in a block format without quotation marks. (See Quotation of Sources, pp. 125–126, and Double or Single Quotation Marks, p. 127, for discussion of block format.)

Do not use double quotation marks

- to identify the anchors of a scale. Instead, italicize them.

  We ranked the items on a scale ranging from 1 (*all of the time*) to 5 (*never*).

- to cite a letter, word, phrase, or sentence as a linguistic example. Instead, italicize the term.

  He clarified the distinction between *farther* and *further*.

- to introduce a technical or key term. Instead, italicize the term.

  The term *zero-base budgeting* appeared frequently in the speech.

- to hedge. Do not use any punctuation with such expressions.

Incorrect:

The teacher "rewarded" the class with tokens.

Correct:

The teacher rewarded the class with tokens.

Parentheses

Use parentheses

- to set off structurally independent elements.

  The patterns were significant (see Figure 5).

  (When a complete sentence is enclosed in parentheses, place punctuation in the sentence inside the parentheses, like this.) If only part of a sentence is enclosed in parentheses (like this), place punctuation outside the parentheses (like this).

- to set off reference citations in text (see Reference Citations in Text, pp. 131–137).

  Dumas and Doré (1991) reported

- to introduce an abbreviation.

  effect on the galvanic skin response (GSR)

- to set off letters that identify items in a series within a sentence or paragraph (see also Seriation, pp. 59–60).

The subject areas included (a) synonyms associated with cultural interactions, (b) descriptors for ethnic group membership, and (c) psychological symptoms and outcomes associated with bicultural adaptation.

- to group mathematical expressions (see also Slash, pp. 37–38, and Equations in Text, p. 75).

  $(k - 1)/(g - 2)$

- to enclose the citation or page number of a direct quotation (see also Citation of Sources, pp. 128–129).

  The author stated, "The effect disappeared within minutes" (Lopez, 1993, p. 311), but she did not say which effect.

  Lopez (1993) found that "the effect disappeared within minutes" (p. 311).

- to enclose numbers that identify displayed formulas and equations.

  $$\mathrm{M}_j = \alpha\mathrm{M}_{j-1} + \mathrm{f}_j + \mathrm{g}_j * \mathrm{g}_{j'} \quad (1)$$

- to enclose statistical values.

  was significant ($p < .05$)

- to enclose degrees of freedom.

  $t(75) = 2.19$

  $F(2, 116) = 3.71$

Do not use parentheses

- to enclose material within other parentheses.

  (the Beck Depression Inventory [BDI]) [the use of brackets avoids nested parentheses]

  was significant, $F(4, 132) = 13.62$, $p < .01$.

- back to back.

  (e.g., defensive pessimism; Norem & Cantor, 1986)

Brackets

Use brackets

- to enclose parenthetical material that is already within parentheses.

  (The results for the control group [$n = 8$] are also presented in Figure 2.)

Exception 1: Do not use brackets if the material can be set off easily with commas without confounding meaning:

Unnecessary:

(as Imai [1990] later concluded)

Better:

(as Imai, 1990, later concluded)

Exception 2: In mathematical material, the placement of brackets and parentheses is reversed; that is, parentheses appear within brackets. (See Equations in Text, p. 75, for further discussion of brackets in equations.)

- to enclose material inserted in a quotation by some person other than the original writer.

  "when [his own and others'] behaviors were studied" (Hanisch, 1992, p. 24)

Do not use brackets

- to set off statistics that already include parentheses.

  was significant, $F(1, 32) = 4.37$, $p < .05$.

not

  was significant, (F[1, 32] = 4.37, $p < .05$).

  was significant, [$F(1, 32) = 4.37$, $p < .05$].

Slash

Use a slash

- to clarify a relationship in which a hyphenated compound is used.

  the classification/similarity-judgment condition

  hits/false-alarms comparison

- to separate numerator from denominator.

  X/Y

- to indicate *per* to separate units of measurement accompanied by a numerical value.

  0.5 deg/s 7.4 mg/kg

but

  luminance is measured in candelas per square meter

- to set off English phonemes.

  /o/

- to cite a republished work in text.

  Freud (1923/1961)

Do not use a slash

- when a phrase would be clearer.

  Each child handed the ball to her mother or guardian.

not

  Each child handed the ball to her mother/guardian.

- for simple comparisons. Use a hyphen or short dash (en dash) instead.

  test–retest reliability

not

  test/retest reliability

- more than once to express compound units. Use centered dots and parentheses as needed to prevent ambiguity.

  $\text{nmol} \cdot \text{hr}^{-1} \cdot \text{mg}^{-1}$

not

  nmol/hr/mg

Spelling

Preferred Spelling

Merriam-Webster's Collegiate Dictionary is the standard spelling reference for APA journals and books. If a word is not in *Webster's Collegiate,* consult the more comprehensive *Webster's Third New International Dictionary.* If the dictionary gives a choice, use the first spelling listed; for example, use *aging* and *canceled* rather than *ageing* and *cancelled.*

Plural forms of some words of Latin or Greek origin can be troublesome; a list of proper and preferred spellings of some of the more common ones follows. Authors are reminded that plural nouns take plural verbs.

Singular	Plural	Singular	Plural
appendix	appendixes	matrix	matrices
cannula	cannulas	phenomenon	phenomena
datum	data	schema	schemas

Hyphenation

Compound words take many forms; that is, two words may be written as (a) two separate words, (b) a hyphenated word, or (c) one unbroken, solid word. Choosing the proper form is sometimes frustrating. For example, is *follow up*, *follow-up*, or *followup* the form to be used? The dictionary is an excellent guide for such decisions, especially for nonscientific words (the term is *follow-up* when functioning as a noun or adjective but *follow up* when functioning as a verb). When a compound can be found in the dictionary, its usage is established and it is known as a *permanent compound* (e.g., *high school*, *caregiver*, and *self-esteem*). Dictionaries do not always agree on the way a compound should be written (open, solid, or hyphenated); APA follows *Webster's Collegiate* in most cases. Compound terms are often introduced into the language as separate or hyphenated words, and as they become more commonplace, they tend to fuse into a solid word. For example, the hyphen was dropped from *life-style* in the 10th edition of *Webster's Collegiate*, and *data base* is now *database*.

There is another kind of compound—the *temporary compound*, which is made up of two or more words that occur together, perhaps only in a particular paper, to express a thought. Because language is constantly expanding, especially in science, temporary compounds develop that are not yet listed in the dictionary. If a temporary compound modifies another word, it may or may not be hyphenated, depending on (a) its position in the sentence and (b) whether the pairing of a compound with another word can cause the reader to misinterpret meaning. The main rule to remember is that if a temporary compound *precedes* what it modifies, it may need to be hyphenated, and if it *follows* what it modifies, it usually does not. If a compound is not in the dictionary, follow the general principles of hyphenation given here and in Table 2.1. When you are still in doubt, use hyphens for clarity rather than omit them. (See also Tables 2.2 and 2.3 for treatment of prefixes.)

General Principle 1

Do not use a hyphen unless it serves a purpose. If a compound adjective cannot be misread or, as with

Table 2.1. Guide to Hyphenating Terms

Rule	Example
Hyphenate	
1. A compound with a participle when it precedes the term it modifies	• role-playing technique • anxiety-arousing condition • water-deprived animals
2. A phrase used as an adjective when it precedes the term it modifies	• trial-by-trial analysis • to-be-recalled items • all-or-none questionnaire
3. An adjective-and-noun compound when it precedes the term it modifies	• high-anxiety group • middle-class families • low-frequency words
4. A compound with a number as the first element when the compound precedes the term it modifies	• two-way analysis of variance • six-trial problem • 12th-grade students
Do not hyphenate	
1. A compound including an adverb ending in *-ly*	• widely used text • relatively homogeneous sample
2. A compound including a comparative or superlative adjective	• better written paper • less informed interviewers • higher scoring students
3. Chemical terms	• sodium chloride solution
4. Foreign phrases used as adjectives or adverbs	• a posteriori test • post hoc comparisons
5. A modifier including a letter or numeral as the second element	• Group B participants • Type II error
6. Common fractions used as nouns	• one third of the participants

many psychological terms, its meaning is established, a hyphen is not necessary.

least squares solution	sex role differences
day treatment program	constant stimulus method
health care reform	repeated measures design
grade point average	heart rate scores

General Principle 2

In a temporary compound that is used as an adjective before a noun, use a hyphen if the term can be misread or if the term expresses a single thought (i.e., all words together modify the noun). For example, are *different word lists* (a) word lists that are different from other

Table 2.2. Prefixes That Do Not Require Hyphens

Prefix	Example	Prefix	Example
after	aftereffect	multi	multiphase
anti	antisocial	non	nonsignificant
bi	bilingual	over	overaggressive
co	coworker	post	posttest
counter	counterbalance	pre	preexperimental
equi	equimax	pro	prowar
extra	extracurricular	pseudo	pseudoscience
infra	infrared	re	reevaluate
inter	interstimulus	semi	semidarkness
intra	intraspecific	socio	socioeconomic
macro	macrocosm	sub	subtest
mega	megawatt	super	superordinate
meta[a]	metacognitive	supra	supraliminal
micro	microcosm	ultra	ultrahigh
mid	midterm	un	unbiased
mini	minisession	under	underdeveloped

[a]But *meta-analysis.*

word lists (if so, *different* modifies *word lists*; thus, write *different word lists*) or (b) lists that present different words (if so, the first word modifies the second, and together they modify *lists*, thus, *different-word lists*). A properly placed hyphen helps the reader understand the intended meaning.

General Principle 3

Most compound adjective rules are applicable only when the compound adjective *precedes* the term it modifies. If a compound adjective *follows* the term, do not use a hyphen, because relationships are sufficiently clear without one.

client-centered counseling

but

the counseling was client centered

t-test results

but

results from *t* tests

General Principle 4

Write most words formed with prefixes as one word (see Table 2.2). Some exceptions, as in Table 2.3, require hyphens.

General Principle 5

When two or more compound modifiers have a common base, this base is sometimes omitted in all except the last modifier, but the hyphens are retained.

long- and short-term memory

2-, 3-, and 10-min trials

Capitalization

Capitalize words—that is, use an uppercase letter for the first letter of a word—according to the guidelines in the following sections.

Words Beginning a Sentence

Capitalize

- the first word in a complete sentence.
- the first word after a colon that begins a complete sentence.

The author made one main point: No explanation that has been suggested so far answers all questions.

Major Words in Titles and Headings

Capitalize

- major words in titles of books and articles within the body of the paper. Conjunctions, articles, and short prepositions are not considered major words; however, capitalize all words of four letters or more. Capitalize all verbs (including linking verbs), nouns, adjectives, adverbs, and pronouns. When a capitalized word is a hyphenated compound, capitalize both words. Also, capitalize the first word after a colon or a dash in a title.

In her book, *History of Pathology*

The criticism of the article, "Long-Term Recidivism"

Table 2.3. Prefixed Words That Require Hyphens

Occurrence	**Example**
Compounds in which the base word is capitalized a number an abbreviation more than one word	• pro-Freudian • post-1970 • pre-UCS trial • non-achievement-oriented students
All *self-* compounds, whether they are adjectives or nouns[a]	• self-report technique • the test was self-paced • self-esteem
Words that could be misunderstood	• re-pair [pair again] • re-form [form again] • un-ionized
Words in which the prefix ends and the base word begins with the same vowel[b]	• meta-analysis • anti-intellectual • co-occur

[a]But *self psychology*.

[b]*Pre* and *re* compounds are usually set solid to base words beginning with *e*.

Exception: In titles of books and articles in reference lists, capitalize only the first word, the first word after a colon or a dash, and proper nouns. Do not capitalize the second word of a hyphenated compound. (See chap. 8 for further discussion of reference style.)

Kalichman, S. C., Kelly, J. A., Hunter, T. L., Murphy, D. A., & Tyler, R. (1993). Culturally tailored HIV-AIDS risk-reduction messages targeted to African-American urban women: Impact on risk sensitization and risk reduction.

- major words in article headings and subheadings.

Exception: In indented paragraph (Level 4) headings, capitalize only the first word and proper nouns (see Levels of Heading, p. 27).

- major words in table titles and figure legends. In table *headings* and figure *captions*, capitalize only the first word and proper nouns (see Headings, pp. 83–85, and Figure Legends and Captions, pp. 115–116).
- references to titles of sections within the same article.

  as explained in the Method section

  which is discussed in the *Data Analyses* subsection

Proper Nouns and Trade Names

Capitalize

- proper nouns and adjectives and words used as proper nouns. Proper adjectives that have acquired a common meaning are not capitalized; consult *Webster's Collegiate* for guidance.

  Freudian slip

  Wilks's lambda

  Greco-Latin square

but

  eustachian tube

  cesarean section

- names of university departments if they refer to a specific department within a specific university and complete names of academic courses if they refer to a specific course.

Department of Sociology, University of Washington

Psychology 101

Developmental Psychopathology

but

a sociology department

an introductory psychology course

- trade and brand names of drugs, equipment, and food.

Elavil [*but* amitriptyline hydrochloride]

Hunter Klockounter

Plexiglas

Do not capitalize names of laws, theories, models, or hypotheses.

the empirical law of effect

associative learning model

but

Gregory's theory of illusions [Retain uppercase in personal names.]

Nouns Followed by Numerals or Letters

Capitalize nouns followed by numerals or letters that denote a specific place in a numbered series.

On Day 2 of Experiment 4

during Trial 5, the no-delay group performed

as shown in Table 2 and Figure 3B

Grant AG02726 from the National Institute on Aging

Exception: **Do not capitalize** nouns that denote common parts of books or tables followed by numerals or letters.

chapter 4

page iv

Do not capitalize nouns that precede a variable.

trial *n* and item *x*

but

Trial 3 and Item b [The number and letter are not variables.]

Titles of Tests

Capitalize exact, complete titles of published and unpublished tests. Words such as *test* or *scale* are not capitalized if they refer to subscales of tests.

Advanced Vocabulary Test

Minnesota Multiphasic Personality Inventory

but

MMPI Depression scale

Do not capitalize shortened, inexact, or generic titles of tests.

a vocabulary test   Stroop color test

Names of Conditions or Groups in an Experiment

Do not capitalize names of conditions or groups in an experiment.

experimental and control groups

participants were divided into information and no-information conditions

but

Conditions A and B [See Nouns Followed by Numerals or Letters, p. 45.]

Names of Factors, Variables, and Effects

Capitalize names of derived factors within a factor analysis. The word *factor* is not capitalized unless it is followed by a number (see Nouns Followed by Numerals or Letters, p. 45).

Mealtime Behavior (Factor 4)

Factors 6 and 7

Big Five personality factors

Do not capitalize effects or variables unless they appear with multiplication signs. (Take care that you do not use the term *factor* when you mean *effect* or *variable*, for example, in an interaction or analysis of variance.)

a significant age effect

the sex, age, and weight variables

but

the Sex × Age × Weight interaction

a 3 × 3 × 2 (Group × Trial × Response) design

a 2 (methods) × 2 (item type)

3 Italicizing and Abbreviating

This chapter presents guidelines on the use of italics and abbreviations for publishing in APA journals. In addition to outlining APA Style and providing examples, the sections include a list of Latin abbreviations and common abbreviations for units of measurement.

Italics

Italicizing Words

For specific use of italics in APA journals, see the guidelines listed below. In general, use italics infrequently.

Use italics for

- titles of books, periodicals, and microfilm publications.

  The Elements of Style

  American Psychologist

- genera, species, and varieties.

  Macaca mulatta

- introduction of a new, technical, or key term or label (after a term has been used once, do not italicize it).

  The term *backward masking*

  box labeled *empty*

- letter, word, or phrase cited as a linguistic example.

  words such as *big* and *little*

  a row of *X*s

- words that could be misread.

  the *small* group [meaning a designation, not group size]

- letters used as statistical symbols or algebraic variables.

  $F(1, 53) = 10.03$

  t test

  trial n

- some test scores and scales.

  Rorschach scores: $F+$ %, Z

  MMPI scales: *Hs*, *Pd*

- periodical volume numbers in reference lists.

  26, 46–67

- anchors of a scale.

  health ratings ranged from 1 (*poor*) to 5 (*excellent*)

Do not use italics for

- foreign phrases and abbreviations common in English (i.e., phrases found as main entries in *Webster's Collegiate Dictionary*).

  a posteriori

  ad lib

  et al.

  vis-à-vis

- chemical terms.

  NaCl, LSD

- trigonometric terms.

  sin, tan, log

- nonstatistical subscripts to statistical symbols or mathematical expressions.

  F_{max}

  $S_{\text{A}} + S_{\text{B}}$, *where* S_{A} *represents Group A's score and* S_{B} *represents Group B's score*

- Greek letters.

  β

- mere emphasis. (Italics are acceptable if emphasis might otherwise be lost; in general, however, use syntax to provide emphasis.)

it is *important* to bear in mind that this process is *not* proposed as a stage theory of developments. [italics are not necessary]

- letters used as abbreviations.

intertrial interval (ITI)

Abbreviations

Use of Abbreviations

To maximize clarity, APA prefers that authors use abbreviations sparingly. Although abbreviations are sometimes useful for long, technical terms in scientific writing, communication is usually garbled rather than clarified if too many are introduced to the reader.

Overuse. Consider whether the space saved by abbreviations in the following sentence justifies the time necessary to master the meaning:

The advantage of the LH was clear from the RT data, which reflected high FP and FN rates for the RH.

Without abbreviations the passage reads as follows:

The advantage of the left hand was clear from the reaction time data, which reflected high false-positive and false-negative rates for the right hand.

Underuse. Excessive use of abbreviations, whether standard or unique to one manuscript, can hinder reading comprehension. Conversely, abbreviations introduced on first mention of a term and used fewer than three times thereafter, particularly in a long paper, may be difficult for a reader to remember, and you probably serve the reader best if you write them out each time. In the following example, however, a standard abbreviation for a long, familiar term eases the reader's task:

Patients at seven hospitals completed the MMPI–2.

Deciding Whether to Abbreviate. In all circumstances other than in the reference list (see APA Reference Style, p. 138) and in the abstract, you must decide (a) whether to spell out a given expression every time it is used in an article or (b) whether to spell it out initially and abbreviate it thereafter. For example, the abbreviations L for large and S for small in a paper discussing different sequences of reward *(LLSS or LSLS)* would be an effective and readily understood shortcut. In another paper, however, writing about the *L reward* and the *S reward* would be both unnecessary and confusing. In most instances, abbreviating experimental group names is ineffective because the abbreviations are not adequately informative or easily recognizable and may even be more cumbersome than the full name. In general, use an abbreviation only (a) if it is conventional or (b) if considerable space can be saved and cumbersome repetition avoided (Reisman, 1962). In short, use only those abbreviations that will help you communicate with your readers. Remember, they have not had the same experience with your abbreviations as you have.

Explanation of Abbreviations

Because the abbreviations that psychologists use in their daily writing may not be familiar to students or to readers in other disciplines or other countries, a term to be abbreviated must, on its first appearance, be written out completely and followed immediately by its abbreviation in parentheses. Thereafter, the abbreviation is used in text without further explanation (do not switch between the abbreviated and written-out forms of a term).

> The results of studies of simple reaction time (RT) to a visual target have shown a strong negative relation between RT and luminance.

Abbreviations in a figure must be explained in the caption or legend. Those in a table must also be explained either in the table title (if it includes words that are abbreviated in the body of the table; see Table Titles, p. 83) or in the table note (see Notes to a Table, pp. 91–94). An abbreviation that is used in several figures or tables must be explained in each figure or table in which the abbreviation is used. Avoid introducing abbreviations into figure captions or table notes if they do not appear in the figure or table. Standard abbreviations for units of measurement do not need to be written out on first use (see Scientific Abbreviations, pp. 54–55).

Abbreviations Accepted as Words

APA Style permits the use of abbreviations that appear as word entries (i.e., that are not labeled *abbr*) in *Webster's Collegiate*. Such abbreviations do not need explanation in text. Examples:

IQ REM ESP AIDS HIV NADP ACTH

Abbreviations Used Often in APA Journals

Some abbreviations are not in the dictionary but appear frequently in the journal for which you are writing. Although probably well understood by many readers, these abbreviations should still be explained when first used. Examples:

Minnesota Multiphasic Personality Inventory (MMPI)

conditioned stimulus (CS)

conditioned avoidance (CA)

intertrial interval (ITI)

consonant–vowel–consonant (CVC)

short-term memory (STM)

reaction time (RT)

Do not use the abbreviations *S*, *E*, or *O* for subject, experimenter, and observer.

Latin Abbreviations

Use the following standard Latin abbreviations only in parenthetical material; in nonparenthetical material, use the English translation of the Latin terms:

cf.	compare	i.e.,	that is
e.g.,	for example	viz.,	namely
, etc.	, and so forth	vs.	versus, against

Exception: Use the abbreviation *v.* (for *versus*) in references and text citations to court cases, whether parenthetical or not.

Exception: In the reference list and in text, use the Latin abbreviation *et al.*, which means "and others," in nonparenthetical as well as parenthetical material.

Scientific Abbreviations

Units of Measurement. Use abbreviations and symbols for metric and nonmetric units of measurement that are accompanied by numeric values (e.g., 4 cm, 30 s, 12 min, 18 hr, 5 lb, 45°).

Units of time: To prevent misreading, do not abbreviate the following units of time, even when they are accompanied by numeric values:

day week month year

A list of some common abbreviations for units of measurement follows.

A, ampere
Å, angstrom
AC, alternating current
a.m., ante meridiem
°C, degree Celsius
Ci, curie
cm, centimeter
cps, cycles per second
dB, decibel (specify scale)
DC, direct current
deg/s, degrees per second
dl, deciliter
°F, degree Fahrenheit
g, gram
g, gravity
hr, hour
Hz, hertz
in., inch (include metric equivalent in parentheses)
IQ, intelligence quotient
IU, international unit
kg, kilogram
km, kilometer
kph, kilometers per hour
kW, kilowatt
L, liter
m, meter
μm, micrometer
mA, milliampere
mEq, milliequivalent
meV, million electron volts
mg, milligram

min, minute
ml, milliliter
mm, millimeter
mM, millimolar
mmHg, millimeters of mercury
mmol, millimole
mol wt, molecular weight
mph, miles per hour (include metric equivalent in parentheses)
ms, millisecond
MΩ, megohm
N, newton
ns, nanosecond
p.m., post meridiem
ppm, parts per million
psi, pounds per square inch (include metric equivalent in parentheses)
rpm, revolutions per minute
s, second
S, siemens
V, volt
W, watt

Abbreviated units of measure need not be repeated when expressing multiple amounts:

16–30 kHz   0.3, 1.5, and 3.0 mg/dl

Write out abbreviations for metric and nonmetric units that are not accompanied by numeric values (e.g., measured in centimeters, several pounds).

Chemical Compounds. Chemical compounds may be expressed by common name or by chemical name. If you prefer to use the common name, provide the chemical name in parentheses on first mention in the Method section. Avoid expressing compounds with chemical formulas, as these are usually less informative to the reader and have a high likelihood of being typed or typeset incorrectly. If names of compounds include Greek letters, retain the letters as symbols and do not write them out (e.g., aspirin or salicylic acid, *not* $C_9H_8O_4$).

Long names of organic compounds are often abbreviated; if the abbreviation is listed as a word entry in *Webster's Collegiate Dictionary* (e.g., NADP for *nicotinamide adenine dinucleotide phosphate*), you may use it freely, without writing it out on first use.

Concentrations. If you express a solution as a percentage concentration instead of as a molar concentration, be sure to specify the percentage as a weight-per-volume ratio (wt/vol), a volume ratio (vol/vol), or a weight ratio (wt/wt) of solute to solvent (Pfaffman, Young, Dethier, Richter, & Stellar, 1954). The higher the concentration is, the more ambiguous the expression as a percentage. Specifying the ratio is especially necessary for concentrations of alcohol, glucose, and sucrose. Specifying the salt form is also essential for precise reporting: *d*-amphetamine HCl or *d*-amphetamine SO4 (note that expression of chemical name in combination with a formula is acceptable in this case).

12% (vol/vol) ethyl alcohol solution

1% (wt/vol) saccharin solution

Routes of Administration. You may abbreviate a route of administration when it is paired with a number-and-unit combination. Preferred style for APA is no periods: icv = intracerebral ventricular, im = intramuscular, ip = intraperitoneal, iv = intravenous, sc = subcutaneous, and so on.

anesthetized with sodium pentobarbital (90 mg/kg ip)

but

the first of two subcutaneous injections (*not* sc injections)

Other Abbreviations

Use abbreviations for statistics as described in chapter 4 (Statistical Symbols, pp. 69–74). For information on the International System of Units (SI), see chapter 4 (Metrication, pp. 65–67).

Use of Periods With Abbreviations

Use the following guide for the use of periods with abbreviations.

Use periods with

- initials of names.
  (J. R. Smith)

- abbreviation for United States when used as an adjective.
  (U.S. Navy)
- identity-concealing labels for study participants.
  (F.I.M.)
- Latin abbreviations.
  (a.m., cf., i.e., vs.)
- reference abbreviations.
  (Vol. 1, 2nd ed., p. 6, F. Supp.)

Do not use periods with

- abbreviations of state names in reference list entries or in vendor locations (e.g., for drugs and apparatus described in the Method section).
  (NY; OH; Washington, DC)
- capital letter abbreviations and acronyms.
  (APA, NDA, NIMH, IQ)
- metric and nonmetric measurement abbreviations.
  (cd, cm, ft, hr, kg, lb, min, ml, s)

  Exception: The abbreviation for inch (in.) takes a period because without the period it could be misread.
- abbreviations for routes of administration.
  (icv, im, ip, iv, sc)

Plurals of Abbreviations

To form the plural of most abbreviations and statistical symbols, add s alone, but not italicized, without an apostrophe.

IQs Eds. vols. *M*s *p*s *n*s

Exception: Do not add an *s* to make abbreviations of units of measurement plural (see Style for Metric Units, pp. 66–67).

Exception: To form the plural of the reference abbreviation p. (page), write pp.; do not add an *s*.

Abbreviations Beginning a Sentence

Never begin a sentence with a lowercase abbreviation (e.g., lb) or a symbol that stands alone (e.g., α). Begin a sentence with a capitalized abbreviation or acronym (e.g., U.S. or APA) or with a symbol connected to a word (e.g., β-Endorphins) only when necessary to avoid indirect and awkward writing. In the case of chemical compounds, capitalize the first letter of the word to which the symbol is connected; keep the locant, descriptor, or positional prefix (i.e., Greek, small capital, and italic letters and numerals) intact.

In running text:

L-methionine

N,*N*′-Dimethylurea

γ-hydroxy-β-aminobutyric acid

At beginning of sentence:

L-Methionine

N,*N*′-Dimethylurea

γ-Hydroxy-β-aminobutyric acid

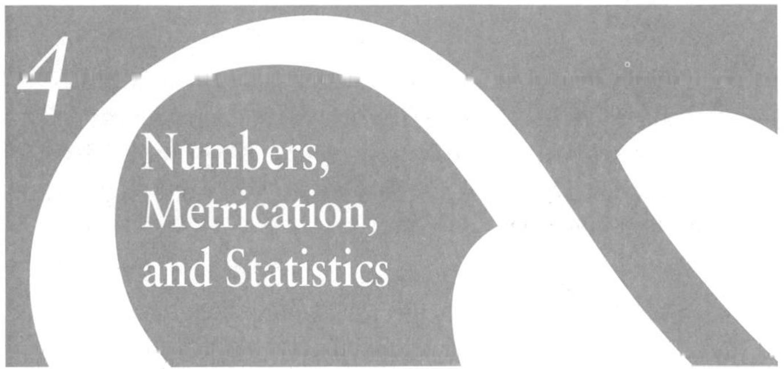

4 Numbers, Metrication, and Statistics

This chapter describes the style for presenting numbers, metrication, and statistics in APA journals. The sections present rules, exceptions, and special usages of numbers; APA's policy on use of the metric system in journals; and guidelines on presenting statistical and mathematical copy.

Numbers

The general rule governing APA Style on the use of numbers is to use figures to express numbers 10 and above and words to express numbers below 10. The next few sections expand on this rule and state exceptions and special usages.

Seriation

Enumerate elements in a series to prevent misreading or to clarify the sequence or relationship between elements, particularly when they are lengthy or complex. Identify the elements by a letter (within a paragraph or sentence) or by a number (at the start of each paragraph in a series).

Within a paragraph or sentence, identify elements in a series by lowercase letters (not italicized) in parentheses.

> The participant's three choices were (a) working with another participant, (b) working with a team, and (c) working alone.

Within a sentence, use commas to separate three or more elements that do not have internal commas; use semicolons to separate three or more elements that have internal commas.

> We tested three groups: (a) low scorers, who scored fewer than 20 points; (b) moderate scorers, who scored between

20 and 50 points; and (c) high scorers, who scored more than 50 points.

If the elements of a series within a paragraph constitute a compound sentence and are preceded by a colon, capitalize the first word of the first item (see Colon, pp. 33–34).

The experiments on which we report were designed to address two such findings: (a) Only a limited class of patterned stimuli, when paired with color, subsequently contingently elicit aftereffects, and (b) decreasing the correlation between grid and color does not degrade the McCollough effect.

Separate paragraphs in a series, such as itemized conclusions or steps in a procedure, are identified by an arabic numeral followed by a period but not enclosed in or followed by parentheses.

Using the learned helplessness theory, we predicted that the depressed and nondepressed participants would make the following judgments of control:

1. Individuals who . . . [paragraph continues].
2. Nondepressed persons exposed to . . . [paragraph continues].
3. Depressed persons exposed to . . . [paragraph continues].
4. Depressed and nondepressed participants in the no-noise groups . . . [paragraph continues].

In any series, with or without enumeration, any item should be syntactically and conceptually parallel to the other items in the series (see Parallel Construction, pp. 17–19).

Numbers Expressed in Figures

Use figures to express

a. all numbers 10 and above. (*Exceptions*: See pp. 62–63.)

12 cm wide	the 15th trial
the remaining 10%	25 years old
10th-grade students	13 lists

b. all numbers below 10 that are grouped for comparison with numbers 10 and above (and that appear in the same paragraph). (*Exceptions*: See pp. 62–63.)

3 of 21 analyses

of 10 conditions . . . the 5th condition

5 and 13 lines

in the 2nd and 11th grades . . . the 2nd-grade students

4 of the 40 stimulus words

toys included 14 balloons, 3 stuffed animals, and 5 balls

but

15 traits on each of four checklists [Traits and checklists are not being compared; they are different categories of items.]

c. numbers that immediately precede a unit of measurement.

a 5-mg dose

with 10.54 cm of

d. numbers that represent statistical or mathematical functions, fractional or decimal quantities, percentages, ratios, and percentiles and quartiles.

multiplied by 5

3 times as many [proportion; cf. p. 62]

0.33 of the

more than 5% of the sample

a ratio of 16:1

the 5th percentile

e. numbers that represent time; dates; ages; sample, subsample, or population size; specific numbers of subjects or participants in an experiment; scores and points on a scale; exact sums of money; and numerals as numerals.

in about 3 years

2 weeks ago

1 hr 34 min

at 12:30 a.m.

March 30, 1994

2-year-olds

3 participants [*but* two raters, seven observers]

9 rats

scored 4 on a 7-point scale

were paid $5 each

the numerals on the scorecard were 0–6

f. numbers that denote a specific place in a numbered series, parts of books and tables, and each number in a list of four or more numbers.

Grade 8 [*but* the eighth grade; see Ordinal Numbers, p. 64]

Trial 3

Table 3

page 71

row 5

1, 3, 4, and 7 words, respectively

g. all numbers in the abstract of a paper except those that begin a sentence.

Numbers Expressed in Words

Use words to express

a. numbers below 10 that do not represent precise measurements and that are grouped for comparison with numbers below 10.

repeated the task three times [cf. p. 61]

the only one who

five trials . . . the remaining seven trials

three conditions

one-tailed *t* test

three-dimensional blocklike figures

six sessions

nine pages

three-way interaction

the third of five taste stimuli

b. the numbers *zero* and *one* when the words would be easier to comprehend than the figures or when the words do not appear in context with numbers 10 and above.

zero-base budgeting

one-line sentence

However, one response was valid. [*but* However, 1 of 15 responses was valid.]

c. any number that begins a sentence, title, or text heading. (Whenever possible, reword the sentence to avoid beginning with a number.)

Ten participants answered the questionnaire

Forty-eight percent of the sample showed an increase; 2% showed no change.

Four patients improved, and 4 patients did not improve.

d. common fractions.

one fifth of the class

two-thirds majority

reduced by three fourths

e. universally accepted usage.

the Twelve Apostles

the Fourth of July

the Ten Commandments

Combining Figures and Words to Express Numbers

Use a combination of figures and words to express

a. rounded large numbers (starting with millions).

almost 3 million people

a budget of $2.5 billion

b. back-to-back modifiers.

2 two-way interactions

ten 7-point scales

twenty 6-year-olds

the first 10 items

A combination of figures and words in these situations increases the clarity and readability of the construction. In some situations, however, readability may suffer instead of benefit. In such a case, spelling out both numbers is preferred.

Poor:

1st two items

first 2 items

Better:

first two items

Ordinal Numbers

Treat ordinal numbers as you would cardinal numbers (see pp. 62–63).

Ordinal	Cardinal base
second-order factor	two orders
the fourth graders	four grades
the first item of the 75th trial	one item, 75 trials
the 2nd and 11th rows	2 rows, 11 rows
the first and third groups	one group, three groups
of 3rd-year students	3 years
4th and 5th years	4 years, 5 years

Decimal Fractions

Use a zero before the decimal point when numbers are less than 1.

0.23 cm, 0.48 s

Do not use a zero before a decimal fraction when the number cannot be greater than 1 (e.g., correlations, proportions, and levels of statistical significance).

$r(24) = -.43$, $p < .05$

The number of decimal places to use in reporting the results of experiments and data analytic manipulations of the data should be governed by three general principles: (a) a fundamental attitude to round as much as possible while keeping (b) prospective use and (c) statistical precision in mind. As a general rule, fewer decimal digits are easier to comprehend than more digits; therefore, in general, it is better to round to two decimal places or to rescale the measurement (in which case effect sizes should be presented in the same metric). For instance, a difference in distances that must be carried to four decimals to be seen when scaled in meters can be more effectively illustrated by conversion to millimeters, which would require only a few decimal digits to illustrate the same difference. As a rule, when properly scaled, most data can be effectively presented with two decimal digits of accuracy. Report correlations, proportions, and inferential statistics such as *t*, *F*, and chi-square to two decimals. In general, significance probabilities will be reported to two decimal places (i.e., the lowest reported significance probability being $p < .01$). There are, however, circumstances under which more decimals may be reported (e.g., Bonferroni tests, exact randomization probabilities).

Roman Numerals

If roman numerals are part of an established terminology, do not change to arabic numerals; for example, use Type II error. Use arabic, not roman, numerals for routine seriation (e.g., Step 1).

Commas in Numbers

Use commas between groups of three digits in most figures of 1,000 or more.

Exceptions:

page numbers	page 1029
binary digits	00110010
serial numbers	290466960
degrees of temperature	3071 °F
acoustic frequency designations	2000 Hz
degrees of freedom	*F*(24, 1000)
numbers to the right of a decimal point	4,900.0744

Plurals of Numbers

To form the plurals of numbers, whether expressed as figures or as words, add s or es alone, without an apostrophe.

fours and sixes   1950s   10s and 20s

Metrication

Policy on Metrication

APA uses the metric system in its journals. All references to physical measurements, where feasible, should be expressed in metric units. The metric system outlined in this section is based, with some exceptions, on the International System of Units (SI), which is an extension and refinement of the traditional metric system and is supported by the national standardizing bodies in many countries, including the United States.

In preparing manuscripts, authors should use metric units if possible. Experimenters who use instruments that record measurements in nonmetric units may report the nonmetric units but also must report the established SI equivalents in parentheses immediately after the nonmetric units.

> The rods were spaced 19 mm apart. [Measurement was made in metric units.]

> The rod was 3 ft (0.91 m) long. [Measurement was made in nonmetric units and converted to the rounded SI equivalent.]

Journal editors reserve the right to return manuscripts if measurements are not expressed properly.

Style for Metric Units

Abbreviation. Use the metric symbol to express a metric unit when it appears with a numeric value (e.g., 4 m). When a metric unit does not appear with a numeric value, spell out the unit in text (e.g., measured in meters), and use the metric symbol in column and stub headings of tables to conserve space (e.g., lag in ms).

Capitalization. Use lowercase letters when writing out full names of units (e.g., meter, nanometer) unless the name appears in capitalized material or at the beginning of a sentence.

For the most part, use lowercase letters for symbols (e.g., cd), even in capitalized material. Symbols derived from the name of a person usually include uppercase letters (e.g., Gy), as do symbols for some prefixes that represent powers of 10: exa (E), peta (P), tera (T), giga (G), and mega (M). (See the list in Scientific Abbreviations, pp. 54–55, for more examples.)

Use the symbol L for liter when it stands alone (e.g., 5 L, 0.3 mg/L) because a lowercase *l* may be misread as the numeral one (use lowercase *l* for fractions of a liter: 5 ml, 9 ng/dl).

Plurals. Make full names of units plural when appropriate. Example: meters

Do not make symbols of units plural. Example: 3 cm, *not* 3 cms

Periods. Do not use a period after a symbol, except at the end of a sentence.

Spacing. Never use a space between a prefix and a base unit. Examples: kg, kilogram

Use a space between a symbol and the number to which it refers, except for measures of angles (e.g., degrees, minutes, and seconds). Examples: 4.5 m, 12 °C, but 45° angle

Compound Units. Use a centered dot between the symbols of a compound term formed by the multiplication of units. Example: Pa · s

Use a space between full names of units of a compound unit formed by the multiplication of units; do not use a centered dot. Example: pascal second

Statistical and Mathematical Copy

APA Style for presenting statistical and mathematical copy reflects both standards of content and form agreed on in the field and the requirements of the printing process.

Selecting the Method of Analysis and Retaining Data

Authors are responsible for the statistical method selected and for all supporting data. Access to computer analyses of data does not relieve the author of responsibility for selecting the appropriate data analytic techniques. To permit interested readers to verify the statistical analysis, an author should retain the raw data after publication of the research. Authors of manuscripts accepted for publication in APA journals are required to have available their raw data throughout the editorial review process and for at least 5 years after the date of publication.

Selecting Effective Presentation

Statistical and mathematical copy can be presented in text, in tables, and in figures. Read References for Statistics (p. 68), chapter 5 (Tables, p. 77), and Deciding to Use Figures (pp. 97–99) to compare methods of presentation and to decide how best to present your data. A general rule that might prove useful is

- if you have 3 or fewer numbers, use a sentence;
- if you have from 4 to 20 numbers, use a table; and
- if you have more than 20 numbers, consider using a graph or figure instead of a table.

When you are in doubt about the clearest and most effective method of presentation, prepare tables or figures with the understanding that if the manuscript is accepted, they are to be published at the editor's discretion. In any case, be prepared to submit tables and figures of complex statistical and mathematical material if an editor requests them.

References for Statistics

Do not give a reference for statistics in common use; this convention applies to most statistics used in journal articles. Do give a reference for (a) less common statistics, especially those that have appeared in journals but that are not yet incorporated in textbooks, or (b) a statistic used in a controversial way (e.g., to justify a test of significance when the data do not meet the assumptions of the test). When the statistic itself is the focus of the article, give supporting references.

Formulas

Do not give a formula for a statistic in common use; do give a formula when the statistic or mathematical expression is new, rare, or essential to the paper. Presentation of equations is described in Equations in Text, page 75, and Displayed Equations, page 75.

Statistics in Text

When reporting inferential statistics (e.g., t tests, F tests, chi-square tests), include sufficient information to allow the reader to fully understand the analyses conducted and possible alternative explanations for the results of these analyses. What constitutes sufficient information depends on the analytic approach selected. Examples of presentations follow:

> For immediate recognition, the omnibus test of the main effect of sentence format was statistically significant, $F(2, 177) = 4.37$, $p = .03$. Regarding the 2 one-degree-of-freedom contrasts of interest (C1 and C2 above), both reached the specified .05 significance level, $F(1, 117) = 4.03$, $p = .05$, and $F(1, 117) = 4.71$, $p = .03$, respectively. In terms of effect sizes . . .

> For the autokinetic movement illusion, as predicted, people highly hypnotizable ($M = 8.19$, $SD = 7.12$) reported perceiv-

ing the stationary light as moving significantly more often than did the other participants (M = 5.26, SD = 4.25), t(60) = 1.99, p = .03 (one-tailed), d = .50. The high-hypnotizability group (M = 21.41, SD = 10.35) reported statistically greater occurrences of extreme, focused attention than did the low group (M = 16.24, SD = 11.09), t(75) = 2.11, p = .02 (one-tailed), d = .48.

If you present descriptive statistics in a table or figure, you do not need to repeat them in text, although highlighting particular data in the narrative may be helpful.

With chi-square, report degrees of freedom and sample size (i.e., the number of independent entries in the chi-square table) in parentheses:

$\chi^2(4, N = 90) = 10.51, p = .03$

When enumerating a series of similar statistics, be certain that the relation between the statistics and their referents is clear. Words such as *respectively* and *in order* can clarify this relationship.

Means (with standard deviations in parentheses) for Trials 1 through 4 were 2.43 (0.50), 2.59 (1.21), 2.68 (0.39), and 2.86 (0.12), respectively.

In order, means for Trials 1 through 4 were 2.43, 2.59, 2.68, and 2.86 (SDs = 0.50, 1.21, 0.39, and 0.12, respectively). The ns for each trial were 17.

Statistical Symbols

When using a statistical term in the narrative, use the term, not the symbol. For example, use The means were, *not* The Ms were.

Symbols for Population Versus Sample Statistics. Population (i.e., theoretical) statistics, properly called *parameters*, are usually represented by lowercase Greek letters. A few sample (i.e., observed) statistics are also expressed by Greek letters (e.g., χ^2), but most sample statistics are expressed by italicized Latin letters (e.g., *SD*).

Symbols for Number of Subjects. Use an uppercase, italicized *N* to designate the number of members in a total sample (e.g., N = 135) and a lowercase, italicized *n* to designate the number of members in a limited portion of the total sample (e.g., n = 30).

Symbol for Percent (%). Use the symbol for percent only when it is preceded by a numeral. Use the word *percentage* when a number is not given.

found that 18% of the rats

determined the percentage of rats

Exception: In table headings and figure legends, use the symbol % to conserve space.

Standard, Boldface, and Italic Type. Statistical symbols and mathematical copy are typeset in three different typefaces: standard, **boldface**, and *italic*. The same typeface is used for a symbol whether the symbol appears in text, tables, or figures.

Greek letters, subscripts, and superscripts that function as identifiers (i.e., that are not variables) and abbreviations that are not variables (e.g., sin, log) are typeset in a standard typeface. On the manuscript, do not italicize them.

μ_{girls}, α, ϵ, β

Symbols for vectors are bold. Use the word processor boldface function (or a handwritten wavy underline).

V

All other statistical symbols are typeset in italic type.

N, M_X, df, p, SS_{b}, SE, MSE, t, F, a, b

A list of common statistical abbreviations is provided in Table 4.1.

Identifying Letters and Symbols. Some letters, numerals, and other characters may be ambiguous to the typesetter and should be clarified with notations embedded in the text on their first appearance in the manuscript (see Equation 1 in Displayed Equations, p. 76). The following characters, for example, may be misread in typewritten copy: 1 (the numeral one or the letter *l*), 0 (the numeral zero or the letter *o*), × (multiplication sign or the letter *x*), Greek letters (the letter *B* or beta), and letters that have the same shape in capital and lowercase forms, which can be especially confusing in subscripts and superscripts (e.g., *c*, *s*, and *x*).

In general, remember that production staff usually do not have mathematical backgrounds and will reproduce what they see, not what a mathematician

Table 4.1. Statistical Abbreviations and Symbols

Abbreviation/ Symbol	Definition
ANCOVA	Analysis of covariance
ANOVA	Analysis of variance (univariate)
d	Cohen's measure of effect size
d'	(d prime) measure of sensitivity
D	Used in Kolmogorov–Smirnov test
df	degree of freedom
f	Frequency
f_e	Expected frequency
F	Fisher's F ratio
F_{max}	Hartley's test of variance homogeneity
g	Hedge's measure of effect size
H	Used in Kruskal–Wallis test; also used to mean *hypothesis*
H_0	Null hypothesis under test
H_1	Alternative hypothesis
HSD	Tukey's honestly significant difference (also referred to as the Tukey *a* procedure)
k	Coefficient of alienation
k^2	Coefficient of nondetermination
K-R 20	Kuder–Richardson formula
LR	Likelihood ratio (used with some chi-squares)
LSD	Fisher's least significant difference
M	Mean (arithmetic average)
MANOVA	Multivariate analysis of variance
Mdn	Median
mle	Maximum likelihood estimate (used with programs such as LISREL)
MS	Mean square
MSE	Mean square error
n	Number in a subsample
N	Total number in a sample

(table continues)

Table 4.1. (continued)

Abbreviation/ Symbol	Definition
ns	Nonsignificant
p	Probability; also the success probability of a binomial variable
P	Percentage, percentile
pr	Partial correlation
q	$1 - p$ for a binomial variable
Q	Quartile (also used in Cochran's test)
r	Pearson product–moment correlation
r^2	Pearson product–moment correlation squared; coefficient of determination
r_b	Biserial correlation
r_k	Reliability of mean *k* judges' ratings
r_1	Estimate reliability of the typical judge
r_{pb}	Point-biserial correlation
r_s	Spearman rank correlation coefficient (formerly rho [ρ])
R	Multiple correlation; also composite rank, a significance test
R^2	Multiple correlation squared; measure of strength of relationship
SD	Standard deviation
SE	Standard error (of measurement)
SEM	Standard error of measurement
SEM	Structural equation modeling
sr	Semipartial correlation
SS	Sum of squares
t	Computed value of *t* test
T	Computed value of Wilcoxon's or McCall's test
T^2	Computed value of Hotelling's test
Tukey *a*	Tukey's HSD procedure
U	Computed value of Mann–Whitney test

Table 4.1. (continued)

Abbreviation/ Symbol	Definition
V	Cramér's statistic for contingency tables; Pillai–Bartlett multivariate criterion
W	Kendall's coefficient of concordance
x	Abscissa (horizontal axis in graph)
y	Ordinate (vertical axis in graph)
z	A standard score; difference between one value in a distribution and the mean of the distribution divided by the *SD*
$\|a\|$	Absolute value of *a*
α	Alpha; probability of a Type I error; Cronbach's index of internal consistency
β	Beta; probability of a Type II error; ($1 - \beta$ is statistical power); standardized multiple regression coefficient
γ	Gamma; Goodman–Kruskal's index of relationship
Δ	Delta (cap); increment of change
κ	Cohen's estimate of effect size
η^2	Eta squared; measure of strength of relationship
Θ	Theta (cap); Roy's multivariate criterion
λ	Lambda; Goodman–Kruskal's measure of predictability
Λ	Lambda (cap); Wilks's multivariate criterion
ν	Nu; degrees of freedom
ρ_I	Rho (with subscript); intraclass correlation coefficient
Σ	Sigma (cap); sum or summation
τ	Tau; Kendall's rank correlation coefficient; also Hotelling's multivariate trace criterion
ϕ	Phi; measure of association for a contingency table; also a parameter used in determining sample size or statistical power
ϕ^2	Phi squared; proportion of variance accounted for in a 2×2 contingency table

(table continues)

Table 4.1. (continued)

Abbreviation/ Symbol	Definition
χ^2	Computed value of a chi-square test
ψ	Psi; a statistical contrast
ω^2	Omega squared; measure of strength of relationship
^	(caret) when above a Greek letter (or parameter), indicates an estimate (or statistic)

Note. Greek symbols are lowercase unless noted otherwise.

knows. If errors appear in the typeset proofs because of ambiguity in a manuscript, the author may be charged for correcting them. Avoid misunderstandings and corrections by preparing mathematical copy carefully and by reviewing the copyedited manuscript thoroughly before returning it to the production office for typesetting.

Spacing, Alignment, and Punctuation

Space mathematical copy as you would space words: $a{+}b{=}c$ is as difficult to read as wordswithoutspacing; $a + b = c$ is much better. Align mathematical copy carefully. Subscripts usually precede superscripts (x_a^2), but a prime is placed next to a letter or symbol (x'_a). Superscripts will be typeset directly above subscripts in APA journals unless the author gives specific instructions to the contrary when transmitting the accepted manuscript for production.

Punctuate all equations, whether they are in the line of text or displayed (i.e., typed on a new line), to conform to their place in the syntax of the sentence (see the period following Equation 1 in Displayed Equations, p. 75). If an equation exceeds the column width of a typeset page (approximately 55 characters, including spaces, will fit on one line in most APA journals), the typesetter will break it. For long equations, indicate on the final version of the accepted manuscript where breaks would be acceptable.

Equations in Text

Place short and simple equations, such as $a = [(1 + b)/x]^{1/2}$, in the line of text. Equations in the line of text should not project above or below the line; for example, the equation above would be difficult to set in the line of text if it were in this form:

$$a = \sqrt{\frac{1 + b}{x}}.$$

To present fractions in the line of text, use a slanted line (/) and appropriate parentheses and brackets: Use ( ) first, then [( )], and finally {[( )]}. Use parentheses and brackets to avoid ambiguity: Does $a/b + c$ mean $(a/b) + c$ or $a/(b + c)$?

Displayed Equations

To display equations, start them on a new line, and double-space twice above and twice below the equation. Simple equations should be displayed if they must be numbered for later reference. Display all complex equations.

Number displayed equations consecutively, with the number in parentheses near the right margin of the page:

(1)

summation zero

(chi) $$\chi = -2\sum a_x^2 + a_0 + \frac{\cos x - 5ab}{1/n + a_x}.$$

(lc ex) (one)

When referring to numbered equations, spell out the reference; for example, write Equation 1 (do not abbreviate as Eq. 1), or write the first equation.

5 Tables

Tables are efficient, enabling the researcher to present a large amount of data in a small amount of space. Tables usually show exact numerical values, and the data are arranged in an orderly display of columns and rows, which aids comparison. For several reasons, it is worthwhile to be selective in choosing how many tables to include in your paper. First, a reader may have difficulty sorting through a large number of tables and may lose track of your message (Scientific Illustration Committee, 1988). Second, a disproportionately large number of tables compared with a small amount of text can cause problems with the layout of typeset pages; text that is constantly broken up with tables will be hard for the reader to follow. Third, tables are complicated to set in type and are therefore more expensive to publish than text. For these reasons, reserve tables for crucial data that are directly related to the content of your article and for simplifying text that otherwise would be dense with numbers.

Dense:

> The mean final errors (with standard deviations in parentheses) for the Age × Level of Difficulty interaction were .05 (.08), .05 (.07), and .11 (.10) for the younger participants and .14 (.15), .17 (.15), and .26 (.21) for the older participants at low, moderate, and high levels of difficulty, respectively.

The reader can more easily comprehend and compare these data when they are presented in tabular form, as in Table Example 1. However, the data in unusually short and simple tables (e.g., a table with two or fewer columns and rows) are more efficiently presented in text.

Determine the amount of data the reader needs to understand the discussion, and then decide whether those data are best presented in text or as a table or fig-

Table Example 1.

Table X

Error Rates of Older and Younger Groups

Level of difficulty	Mean error rate		Standard deviation		Sample size	
	Younger	Older	Younger	Older	Younger	Older
Low	.05	.14	.08	.15	12	18
Moderate	.05	.17	.07	.15	15	12
High	.11	.26	.10	.21	16	14

Table Example 2.

Table X

Mean Numbers of Correct Responses by Children With and Without Pretraining

	Girls			Boys		
Grade	With	Without	Difference	With	Without	Difference
			Verbal tests			
3	280	240	40	281	232	49
4	297	251	46	290	264	26
5	301	260	41	306	221	85
n[a]	18	19		19	20	
			Mathematical tests			
3	201	189	12	210	199	11
4	214	194	20	236	210	26
5	221	216[b]	5	239	213	26
n[a]	20	17		19	18	

Note. Maximum score = 320.

[a]Numbers of children out of 20 in each group who completed all tests.

[b]One girl in this group gave only two correct responses.

STUBHEAD · COLUMN SPANNER · DECKED HEADS · TABLE SPANNER · COLUMN HEADS · CELL · STUB · TABLE SPANNER · TABLE BODY · NOTES TO TABLE

ure. Peripherally related or extremely detailed data should be omitted or, depending on their nature, presented in an appendix (see Appendixes, pp. 122–124).

Tables usually present quantitative data. Occasionally, however, a table that consists of words is used to present qualitative comparisons. For additional information on word tables, see Presenting Data in Specific Types of Tables, pages 86–90.

Tables that communicate quantitative data are effective only when the data are arranged so that their meaning is obvious at a glance (Ehrenberg, 1977; Wainer, 1997). A table should be organized so that entries that are to be compared are next to one another. Following this principle, it is generally the case that different indices (e.g., means, standard deviations, sample sizes) should be segregated into different parts of tables. Table Example 1 illustrates these principles. An author's thoughtful preparation can result in tables that very effectively communicate the essential results of an empirical inquiry.

Table Example 2 shows the basic elements of a table and illustrates the advantage of including derivative values in a table—in this case, the differences between the *With* and *Without Pretraining* subsamples that are the focus of the discussion. Detailed information on the preparation of tables is presented in the remaining sections of this chapter. Table Examples 3 and 4 are

Table Example 3.

Table X
Mean Causality and Responsibility Attribution Scores

Personal similarity	Situational similarity: Low	Situational similarity: High
	Causality	
High	16	15
Low	32	20
	Responsibility	
High	16	9
Low	38	19

Note. The higher the score, the greater the attribution. Actual scores have been multiplied by 10.

Table Example 4.

Table X

Recognition Memory for Words and Nonwords as a Function of Age and Viewing Condition

Viewing condition	Adults[a]	Children[b]	Difference
		Words	
Dim	91	73	18
Moderate	88	63	25
Bright	61	45	16
		Nonwords	
Dim	78	58	20
Moderate	65	62	3
Bright	80	51	29

Note. The values represent mean percentages of correctly recognized words or nonwords.

[a]Adults were 18–21 years old. [b]Children were 12–14 years old.

examples of different kinds of tables as they would appear in a manuscript, that is, as typed. These tables show the proper form and arrangement of titles, headings, data in the body of the table, footnotes, and rules.

Many data tables have certain canonical forms. The advantage of using the canonical form is that the reader generally knows where to look in the table for certain kinds of information. Table Example 5 presents the canonical form for reporting correlations in two groups. There are situations, however, where presentation in noncanonical form can enhance the reader's understanding of the point being made. Consider, for example, the same data recast into Table Example 6. In this case a number of changes have been made in the form of the table; most noticeably, the order of the variables in the rows and columns is not the same. The column order has been rearranged to bring the high positive correlations together, thereby making the structure of the relationships clearer. In addition, the nonmeaningful correlations of the variable with itself have been eliminated, and the number of decimals has been reduced so that the

Table Example 5. Sample correlation table

Table X

Intercorrelations Between Subscales for Students and Older Adults

Subscale	1	2	3	4
	Students (*n* = 200)			
1. Tranquillity	—	.93	−.09	.73
2. Goodwill		—	−.34	.62
3. Happiness			—	.14
4. Elation				—
	Older adults (*n* = 189)			
1. Tranquillity	—	.42	−.07	.52
2. Goodwill		—	−.43	.62
3. Happiness			—	.47
4. Elation				—

Table Example 6.

Table X

Intercorrelations Between Subscales for Students and Older Adults

Subscale	Goodwill	Elation	Happiness
	Students (*n* = 200)		
Tranquillity	.9	.7	−.1
Goodwill		.6	−.3
Elation			.1
	Older adults (*n* = 189)		
Tranquillity	.4	.5	−.1
Goodwill		.6	−.4
Elation			.5

essential features of the data are stressed (but at the cost of some detail and precision). The judicious use of noncanonical forms can be effective but must always be motivated by the special circumstances of the data array.

Additional information on ways to present data in specific kinds of tables is presented on pages 86–89 (see also Nicol & Pexman, 1999).

Relation of Tables and Text

Discussing Tables in Text

An informative table supplements—instead of duplicates—the text. In the text, refer to every table and tell the reader what to look for. Discuss only the table's highlights; if you discuss every item of the table in text, the table is unnecessary.

Ensuring That Each Table Can Be Understood on Its Own

Each table should be an integral part of the text but also should be intelligible without reference to the text. Explain all abbreviations (except such standard statistical abbreviations as *M*, *SD*, and *df*) and special use of underlining, dashes, and parentheses. Always identify units of measurement.

Citing Tables

In the text, refer to tables by their numbers:

as shown in Table 8, the responses were . . .

children with pretraining (see Table 5) . . .

Do not write "the table above" (or below) or "the table on page 32," because the position and page number of a table cannot be determined until the typesetter sets the pages.

Relation Between Tables

Consider combining tables that repeat data. Ordinarily, identical columns or rows of data should not appear in two or more tables. Be consistent in the presentations of all tables within a paper to facilitate comparisons. Use similar formats, titles, and headings, and use the same terminology throughout (e.g., *response time* or *reaction time*, not both).

Table Numbers

Number all tables with arabic numerals in the order in which the tables are first mentioned in text (Table 1, Table 2), regardless of whether a more detailed discussion of the tables occurs later in the paper (the typesetter lays out tables and figures closest to where they are first mentioned). If the manuscript includes an appendix with tables, identify the tables of the appendix with capital letters and arabic numerals (e.g., Table A1 is the first table of Appendix A or of a sole appendix, which is not labeled with a letter; Table C2 is the second table of Appendix C).

Table Titles

Give every table a brief but clear and explanatory title.

Too telegraphic:

> *Relation Between College Majors and Performance* [It is unclear what data are presented in the table.]

Too detailed:

> *Mean Performance Scores on Test A, Test B, and Test C of Students With Psychology, Physics, English, and Engineering Majors* [This duplicates information in the headings of the table.]

Good title:

> *Mean Performance Scores of Students With Different College Majors*

Abbreviations that appear in the headings or the body of a table sometimes can be parenthetically explained in the table title. For example,

> *Hit and False-Alarm (FA) Proportions in Experiment 2*

Abbreviations that require longer explanations or that do not relate to the table title are explained in a general note to the table (see Notes to a Table, pp. 91–94). Do not use a specific footnote to clarify an element of the title.

Headings

A table classifies related items and enables the reader to compare them. Data form the body of the table. Headings establish the logic of your organization of the data and identify the columns of data beneath them. Like a table title, a heading should be telegraphic and should not be many more characters in length than the widest entry of the column it spans. For example,

Poor:

Grade level
3
4
5

Better:

Grade
3
4
5

You may use standard abbreviations and symbols for nontechnical terms (e.g., *no.* for *number*, % for *percent*) and for statistics (e.g., *M*, *SD*, χ^2) in table headings without explanation. Abbreviations of technical terms, group names, and the like must be explained in a note to the table (see Notes to a Table, pp. 91–94).

Each column of a table must have a heading, including the *stub column*, or leftmost column of the table (its heading is called the *stub head*). The stub column usually lists the major independent variables. In Table Example 2, for example, the stub lists the grades. Number elements only when they appear in a correlation matrix (see Table Example 5) or if the text refers to them by number.

Subordination within the stub is easier to comprehend by indenting stub items instead of by creating an additional column. This also simplifies the typesetting by keeping the number of columns to a minimum.

Poor:

Sex	Pretraining
Girls	With
	Without
Boys	With
	Without

Better:

Group
Girls
With
Without
Boys
With
Without

All headings identify items below them, not across from them. The headings just above the body of the table (called *column heads* and *column spanners*) identify the entries in the vertical columns in the body of the table. A column head covers just one column; a column spanner covers two or more columns, each with its own column head. Headings stacked in this way are called *decked heads*. Often decked heads can be used to avoid repetition of words in column headings (see Table Example 2). If possible, do not use more than two levels of decked heads.

Incorrect:

Temporal lobe:	Left	Right

Wordy:

Left temporal lobe	Right temporal lobe

Correct:

Temporal lobe	
Left	Right

A few tables may require *table spanners* in the body of the table. These table spanners cover the entire width of the body of the table, allowing for further divisions within the table (see Table Example 2). Also, table spanners can be used to combine two tables into one, provided they have similar column heads.

Any item within a column should be syntactically as well as conceptually comparable with the other items in that column, and all items should be described by the heading:

Nonparallel:

Condition
Functional psychotic
Drinks to excess
Character disorder

Parallel:

Condition
Functional psychosis
Alcoholism
Character disorder

Stubheads, column heads, and column spanners should be singular unless they refer to groups (e.g., *Children*), but table spanners may be plural. Use sentence style for capitalization: Capitalize only the first letter of the first word of all headings (column headings, column spanners, stub heads, and table spanners) and word entries. (All proper nouns should be in caps and lowercase.)

Body of a Table

Decimal Values

The body of a table contains the data. Express numerical values in the number of decimal places that the precision of measurement justifies (see Decimal Fractions, pp. 64–65), and, if possible, carry all comparable values to the same number of decimal places. Do not change the unit of measurement or the number of decimal places within a column.

Empty Cells

If the point of intersection between a row and a column (called a *cell*) cannot be filled because data are not applicable, leave the cell blank. If a cell cannot be filled because data were not obtained or are not reported, insert a dash in that cell and explain the use of the dash in the general note to the table. By convention, a dash in a correlation matrix (see Table Example 5) usually indicates that the correlation of an item with itself was not computed. No explanation of this use of the dash in a correlation matrix is needed. If you need to explain that data in a correlation matrix are unavailable, unreported, or inapplicable, use a specific note (see Notes to a Table, pp. 91–94) rather than a dash.

Conciseness

Be selective in your presentation. Do not include columns of data that can be calculated easily from other columns:

Not concise:

	No. responses			
Participant	First trial	Second trial	Total	*M*
1	5	7	12	6

The example could be improved by (a) giving either the number of responses per trial or the total number of responses, whichever is more important to the discussion, and (b) not including the column of averages because their calculation is simple.

Presenting Data in Specific Types of Tables

Analysis of Variance (ANOVA) Tables

To avoid statistics-laden text that is difficult to read, you may want to present ANOVA statistics in a table. To do so, list the source in the stub column, degrees of freedom in the next column, and the *F* ratios next (mark statistically significant values with asterisks).

Stub entries should first show between-subjects variables and the error and then within-subject variables and any error. Enclose mean square errors in parentheses, and explain them in a general note to the table. Provide the probability values in a probability footnote (see Notes to a Table, pp. 91–94); avoid columns of probability values (see Table Example 7).

Regression Tables

List both raw or unstandardized (*B*) and standardized beta (β) coefficients unless the study is purely applied (in which case, list only *B*s) or purely theoretical (in which case, list only βs). Specify in the table whether you used hierarchical or simultaneous analysis. For hierarchical regressions, be sure to provide the increments of change (see Table Example 8).

Table Example 7. Sample ANOVA table

Table X

Analysis of Variance for Classical Conditioning

Source	*df*	*F*	η	*p*
	Between subjects			
Anxiety (A)	2	0.76	.22	.48
Shock (S)	1	0.01	.02	.92
A × S	2	0.18	.11	.84
S within-group error	30	(16.48)		
	Within subjects			
Blocks (B)	4	3.27**	.31	.01
B × A	8	0.93	.24	.49
B × S	4	2.64*	.28	.04
B × A × S	8	0.58	.19	.79
B × S within-group error	120	(1.31)		

Note. Values enclosed in parentheses represent mean square errors. S = subjects. Adapted from "The Relation of Drive to Finger-Withdrawal Conditioning," by M. F. Elias, 1965, *Journal of Experimental Psychology, 70,* p. 114.

$^*p < .05$. $^{**}p < .01$.

Table Example 8. Sample regression table

Table X

Summary of Hierarchical Regression Analysis for Variables Predicting Adult Daughters' Belief in Paternalism (N = 46)

Variable	*B*	*SE B*	β
Step 1			
Daughter's education	−5.89	1.93	−.41*
Mother's age	0.67	0.31	.21*
Step 2			
Daughter's education	−3.19	1.81	−.22
Mother's age	0.31	0.28	.14
Attitude toward elders	1.06	0.28	.54*
Affective feelings	1.53	0.60	.31*
Dogmatism	−0.03	0.10	−.04

Note. R^2 = .26 for Step 1; ΔR^2 = .25 for Step 2 (*p*s < .05). From "Relationship of Personal–Social Variables to Belief in Paternalism in Parent Caregiving Stiuations," by V. G. Cicirelli, 1990, *Psychology and Aging, 5,* 436. Copyright 1990 by the American Psychological Association. Adapted with permission of the author.

*$p < .05$.

Path and LISREL (Linear Structural Relations) Tables

Present the means, standard deviations, and intercorrelations of the entire set of variables you use as input to path and LISREL analyses. These data are essential for the reader to replicate or confirm your analyses and are necessary for archival purposes, for example, if your study is included in meta-analyses. To help the reader interpret your table, give short descriptions instead of just a list of symbols of the *x* and *y* variables used in the models (see Table Example 9). If you need to use acronyms, be sure to define each one.

Occasionally, multiple models are compared in LISREL analyses. In cases like these, it may be useful to summarize the fit of these models and tests of model comparisons (see Table Example 10). (Results of analyses of structural models are often presented in a figure; see Types of Figures, pp. 99–105.)

Table Example 9. Sample LISREL table

Table X

Factor Loadings and Uniqueness for Confirmatory Factor Model of Type A Behavior Pattern Variables

Measure and variable	Unstandardized factor loading	*SE*	Uniqueness
SI—Speech Characteristics			
Loud and explosive	.60	—	.32
Response latency	.71	.04	.16
Verbal competitiveness	.82	.05	.25
SI—Answer Content			
Competitiveness	.60	—	.34
Speed	.59	.04	.27
Impatience	.67	.05	.28
SI—Hostility			
Stylistic rating	.60	—	.22
Content rating	.60	.05	.17
Thurstone Activity Scale			
Variable 1	.60	—	.73
Variable 2	.88	.08	.39
Variable 3	.71	.07	.54

Note. Dashes indicate the standard error was not estimated. SI = Structured Interview. From "The Nomological Validity of the Type A Personality Among Employed Adults," by D. C. Ganster, J. Schaubroeck, W. E. Sime, and B. T. Mayes, 1991, *Journal of Applied Psychology, 76,* p. 154. Copyright 1991 by the American Psychological Association. Adapted with permission of the author.

Word Tables

Unlike most tables, which present quantitative data, some tables consist mainly of words. Word tables present qualitative comparisons or descriptive information. For example, a word table can enable the reader to compare characteristics of studies in an article that reviews many studies, or it can present questions and responses from a survey or show an outline of the elements of a theory. Word tables illustrate the discussion in the text; they should not repeat the discussion (see Table Example 11).

Word tables include the same elements of format as do other types of tables—table number and title, headings, rules, and possibly notes. Keep column entries brief and simple. Indent any runover lines in entries. *Double-space all parts of a word table.*

Table Example 10. Sample model comparison table

Table X

Fit Indices for Nested Sequence of Cross-Sectional Models

Model	χ^2	NFI	PFI	χ^2_{diff}	ΔNFI
1. Mobley's (1977) measurement model	443.18*	.92	.67		
2. Quit & search intentions	529.80*	.89	.69		
Difference between Model 2 & Model 1				86.61*	.03
3. Search intentions & thoughts of quitting	519.75*	.90	.69		
Difference between Model 3 & Model 1				76.57*	.02
4. Intentions to quit & thoughts of quitting	546.97*	.89	.69		
Difference between Model 4 & Model 1				103.78*	.03
5. One withdrawal cognition	616.97*	.87	.70		
Difference between Model 5 & Model 1				173.79*	.05
6. Horn et al.'s (1984) structural model	754.37*	.84	.71		
Difference between Model 6 & Model 5				137.39*	.03
7. Structural null model	2,741.49*	.23	.27		
Difference between Model 7 & Model 6				1,987.13*	.61
8. Null model	3,849.07*				

Note. NFI = normed fit index; PFI = parsimonious fit index. From "Structural Equations Modeling Test of a Turnover Theory: Cross-Sectional and Longitudinal Analyses," by P. W. Horn and R. W. Griffeth, 1991, *Journal of Applied Psychology, 76,* p. 356. Copyright 1991 by the American Psychological Association. Reprinted with permission of the author. $^*p < .05$.

Notes to a Table

Tables have three kinds of notes, which are placed below the table: general notes, specific notes, and probability notes.

A general note qualifies, explains, or provides information relating to the table as a whole and ends with an explanation of abbreviations, symbols, and the like.

General notes are designated by the word *Note* (italicized) followed by a period. (See Tables From Another Source, p. 95, and Table Examples 7–11 for examples of general notes indicating that a table is from another source.)

Note. All nonsignificant three-way interactions were omitted. M = match process; N = nonmatch process.

A specific note refers to a particular column, row, or individual entry. Specific notes are indicated by superscript lowercase letters (e.g., [a], [b], [c]). Within the headings and table body, order the superscripts from left to right and from top to bottom, starting at the top left. Specific notes to a table do not apply to any other table, and each table's first footnote begins with a superscript lowercase *a*. (See Table Examples 2 and 4 for examples of this kind of note.)

[a]$n = 25$. [b]This participant did not complete the trials.

A probability note indicates the results of tests of significance. Asterisks indicate those values for which the null hypothesis is rejected, with the probability (p value) specified in the probability note. Include a probability note only when relevant to specific data within the table. Assign a given alpha level the same number of asterisks from table to table within your paper, such as $^{*}p < .05$ and $^{**}p < .01$; the largest probability receives the fewest asterisks.

$F(1, 52)$
6.95*
12.38**

$^{*}p < .05$. $^{**}p < .01$.

Ordinarily, you will use asterisks to identify probability values; occasionally, however, you may need to distinguish between one-tailed and two-tailed tests in the

Table Example 11. Sample word table

Table X

Some Memorial and Processing Advantages of the Fuzzy-Processing Preference

Advantage	Description
Trace availability	Gist has a memorial stability advantage over verbatim detail; reasoning operates on types of information available in memory.
Trace accessibility	Retrieval advantage: Gist can be accessed by a broader range of retrieval cues than verbatim traces.
Trace malleability	Schematic, patternlike nature makes gist easier to manipulate than verbatim traces during reasoning.
Processing simplicity	Simpler representations call for simpler processing operations, and gist is simpler than verbatim traces.
Processing effort	The fuzzy-processing preference comports with the law of least effort: Reasoning gravitates toward processing activities that are easier to execute.

Note. From "Memory Independence and Memory Interference in Cognitive Development," by C. J. Brainerd and V. F. Reyna, 1993, *Psychological Review, 100,* p. 48. Copyright 1993 by the American Psychological Association. Adapted with permission of the author.

same table. To do so, use asterisks for the two-tailed *p* values and an alternate symbol (e.g., daggers) for the one-tailed *p* values.

$^{*}p < .05$, two-tailed. $^{**}p < .01$, two-tailed.
$^{\dagger}p < .05$, one-tailed. $^{\dagger\dagger}p < .01$, one-tailed.

Asterisks attached to the obtained value of a statistical test in a table indicate probability. To indicate significant differences between two or more table entries—for example, means that are compared with procedures such as a Tukey test—use lowercase *sub*scripts (see Table Example 12). Explain the use of the subscripts in the table note (see the following sample table notes).

Note. Means having the same subscript are not significantly different at $p < .01$ in the Tukey honestly significant difference comparison.

or

Note. Means with different subscripts differ significantly at $p < .01$ by the Fisher least significant difference test.

Order the notes to a table in the following sequence: *general* note, *specific* note, *probability* note.

Note. The participants . . . responses.

[a]$n = 25$. [b]$n = 42$.

*$p < .05$. **$p < .01$.

Each type of note begins flush left (i.e., no paragraph indentation) on a new line below the table and is double-spaced. The first *specific* note begins flush left on a new line under the *general* note; subsequent specific notes follow one after the other on the same line (lengthy specific notes may be set on separate lines when typeset). The first *probability* note begins flush left on a new line; subsequent probability notes are run in.

Notes are useful for eliminating repetition from the body of a table. Certain types of information may be

Table Example 12. Sample of data comparison

Table X

Judgments of Agency of Life Events by Condition

	Anger		Sadness	
Target judgment	Hot	Cold	Hot	Cold
Future problems	4.10_a	4.35_a	5.46_b	3.81_a
Future successes	4.31_a	4.55_a	4.55_a	3.85_a
Life circumstances	3.80_a	4.50_b	5.40_c	3.46_a

Note. Judgments were made on 9-point scales (1 = *completely due to people's actions*, 9 = *completely due to impersonal forces*). Means in the same row that do not share subscripts differ at $p < .05$ in the Tukey honestly significant difference comparison. From "Beyond Simple Pessimism: Effects of Sadness and Anger on Social Perception," by D. Keltner, P. C. Ellsworth, and K. Edwards, 1993, *Journal of Personality and Social Psychology, 64,* p. 751. Copyright 1993 by the American Psychological Association. Adapted with permission of the author.

appropriate either in the table or in a note. To determine the placement of such material, remember that clearly and efficiently organized data enable the reader to focus on the significance of the data. Thus, if probability values or subsample sizes are numerous, use a column rather than many notes. Conversely, if a row or column contains few entries (or the same entry), eliminate the column by adding a note to the table:

Poor:

Group	*n*
Anxious	15
Depressed	15
Control	15

Better:

Group[a]
Anxious
Depressed
Control

[a]$n = 15$ for each group.

Ruling of Tables

Typesetting requirements restrict the use of rules (i.e., lines) in a table. Limit the rules to those that are necessary for clarity, and use horizontal rather than vertical rules. (Vertical rules are rarely used in APA journals.) Appropriately positioned white space can be an effective substitute for rules; for example, long, uninterrupted columns of numbers or words are more readable if a horizontal line of space is inserted after every fourth or fifth entry.

In the manuscript, use generous spacing between columns and rows and strict alignment to clarify relationships within a table.

Size of Tables

Turning a journal sideways to read a table is an inconvenience to readers. You can design a table to fit the width of a journal page or column if you count characters (i.e., letters, numbers, and spaces). Count characters in the widest entry in each column (whether in the table body or in a heading), and allow 3 characters for spaces between columns. If the count exceeds 60, the table will not fit across the width of most APA journal columns. If the count exceeds 125, the table will not fit across the width of most APA journal pages. To determine the fit, count the characters that fit across a column or page in the journal for which you are writing, and adjust your table if necessary. When typing tables, it is acceptable to turn them sideways (landscape orientation for setting up a laser printer) on the page or run them over several pages, but do not single-space or reduce the type size.

Tables From Another Source

Authors must obtain permission to reproduce or adapt all or part of a table (or figure) from a copyrighted source. It is not necessary to obtain permission from APA to reproduce one table (or figure) from an APA article provided you obtain the author's permission and give full credit to APA as copyright holder and to the author through a complete and accurate citation. When you wish to reproduce material from sources not copyrighted by APA, contact the copyright holders to determine their requirements for both print and electronic reuse. If you have any doubt about the policy of the copyright holder, you should request permission. Always enclose the letter of permission when transmitting the final version of the accepted manuscript for production.

Any reproduced table (or figure) must be accompanied by a note at the bottom of the reprinted table (or in the figure caption) giving credit to the original author and to the copyright holder. If the table (or figure) contains test items, see the cautionary note in Tests and Questionnaires, pages 123–124. Use the following form for tables or figures. (For copyright permission footnotes in text [see Permission to Quote, pp. 129–130], use the following form, but substitute the indented superscript footnote number for the word *Note*.)

Material reprinted from a journal article:

> *Note*. From [*or* The data in column 1 are from] "Title of Article," by A. N. Author and C. O. Author, 2000, *Title of Journal, 50,* p. 22. Copyright 2000 by the Name of Copyright Holder. Reprinted [*or* Adapted] with permission.

Material reprinted from a book:

> *Note*. From [*or* The data in column 1 are from] *Title of Book* (p. 103), by A. N. Author and C. O. Author, 1999, Place of Publication: Publisher. Copyright 1999 by the Name of Copyright Holder. Reprinted [*or* Adapted] with permission.

Table Checklist

- Is the table necessary?
- Is the entire table—including the title, headings, and notes—double-spaced?
- Are all comparable tables in the manuscript consistent in presentation?
- Is the title brief but explanatory?
- Does every column have a column heading?
- Are all abbreviations; special use of italics, parentheses, and dashes; and special symbols explained?
- Are all probability level values correctly identified, and are asterisks attached to the appropriate table entries? Is a probability level assigned the same number of asterisks in all tables in the same article?
- Are the notes in the following order: general note, specific note, probability note?
- Are all vertical rules eliminated?
- Will the table fit across the width of a journal column or page?
- If all or part of a copyrighted table is reproduced, do the table notes give full credit to the copyright owner? Have you received written permission for reuse (in print and electronic form) from the copyright holder and sent a copy with the final version of your paper?
- Is the table referred to in text?

This chapter provides an overview of the use of figures in APA journals. Sections include information on basic types of figures, the preparation of figures, how to create graphs, how to use photographs, and figure legends and captions. A useful Figure Checklist is also included.

Deciding to Use Figures

In APA journals, any type of illustration other than a table is called a *figure*. (Because tables are typeset, rather than photographed from artwork supplied by the author, they are not considered figures.) A figure may be a chart, graph, photograph, drawing, or other depiction.

Consider carefully whether to use a figure. Tables are often preferred for the presentation of quantitative data in archival journals because they provide exact information; figures typically require the reader to estimate values. On the other hand, figures convey at a quick glance an overall pattern of results. They are especially useful in describing an interaction—or lack thereof—and nonlinear relations. A well-prepared figure can also convey structural or pictorial concepts more efficiently than can text (for guidelines on displaying data in figures, see Nicol & Pexman, 2003).

During the process of drafting a manuscript, and in deciding whether to use a figure, ask yourself these questions:

- What idea do you need to convey?
- Is the figure necessary? If it duplicates text, it is not necessary. If it complements text or eliminates lengthy discussion, it may be the most efficient way to present the information.

- What type of figure (e.g., graph, chart, diagram, drawing, map, or photograph) is most suited to your purpose? Will a simple, relatively inexpensive figure (e.g., line art) convey the point as well as an elaborate, expensive figure (e.g., photographs combined

Figure Example 1. Sample line graph.[1]

- Lines are smooth and sharp.
- Typeface is simple (sans serif) and legible.
- Unit of measure is indicated in axis label.
- Axis labels are shared by both panels to decrease clutter.
- Legends are contained within the borders of the graph.
- Symbols are easy to differentiate.
- Caption explains error bars.

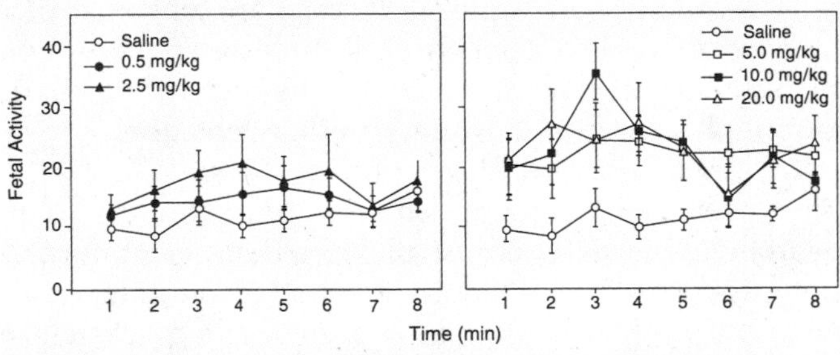

Figure X. Overall motor activity during the first 8 min of the observation session of E21 (Embryonic Day 21) rat fetuses treated with isotonic saline or varying dosages of cocaine. Cocaine groups in the left panel did not differ significantly from the saline-treated control group; cocaine groups in the right panel exhibited significantly elevated activity compared with the control group. Points represent the mean number of movements per minute; vertical lines depict standard errors of the means.

[List captions together on a separate page.]

[1]From "Cocaine Alters Behavior in the Rat Fetus," by D. K. Simonik, S. R. Robinson, and W. P. Smotherman, 1993, *Behavioral Neuroscience, 107,* p. 870. Copyright 1993 by the American Psychological Association.

with line art, figures that are in color instead of in black and white)?

Standards for Figures

The standards for good figures are simplicity, clarity, and continuity. A good figure augments rather than duplicates the text; conveys only essential facts; omits visually distracting detail; is easy to read—its elements (type, lines, labels, symbols, etc.) are large enough to be read with ease in the printed form; is easy to understand—its purpose is readily apparent; is consistent with and is prepared in the same style as similar figures in the same article; that is, the lettering is of the same size and typeface, lines are of the same weight, and so forth; and is carefully planned and prepared.

Types of figures and guidelines for preparing them are described in the following sections so that you can select the figure most appropriate to the information being presented and ensure the preparation of a figure of professional quality. If you engage a professional artist, supply the artist with the guidelines in this section.

Types of Figures

Several types of figures can be used to present data to the reader. Figure Examples 1 through 4 show that

Figure Example 2. Alternative line graph to left panel of previous figure.

- Expanding the scale makes differences within the data more visible.
- A single error bar shows the only significant difference.

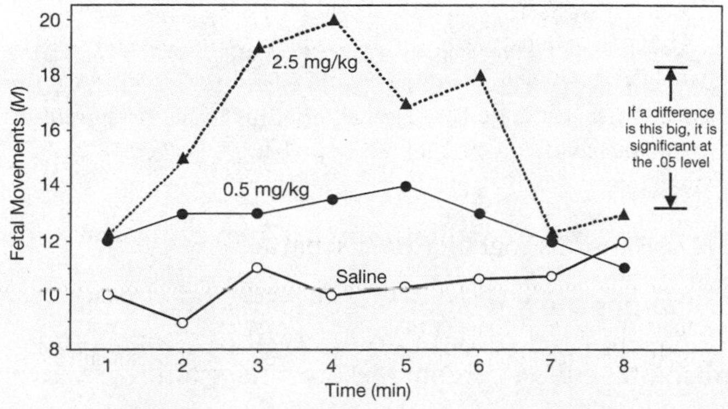

Figure Example 3. Sample bar graph.[2]

- Bars are easy to differentiate by fill pattern.
- Zero point is indicated on ordinate axis.
- Axes are labeled with legible type; ordinate axis indicates unit of measure.
- Legend appears within dimensions of the graph.
- Axes are just long enough to accommodate bar length.
- Caption explains error bars and sample sizes.

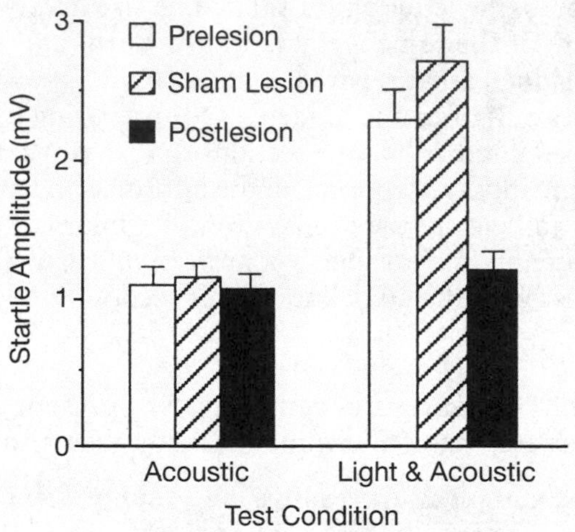

Figure X. Mean amplitude startle response (+ *SE*) for prelesion (*n* = 4), sham lesion (*n* = 2), and postlesion (*n* = 2) groups in acoustic and light-and-acoustic test conditions.

[List captions together on a separate page.]

---

[2]From "Amygdala Efferents Mediating Electrically Evoked Startle-Like Responses and Fear Potentiation of Acoustic Startle," by J. S. Yeomans and B. A. Pollard, 1993, *Behavioral Neuroscience, 107,* p. 606. Copyright 1993 by the American Psychological Association. Adapted with permission of the author.

there are different methods for depicting the same data in a figure.

Graphs show relations—comparisons and distributions—in a set of data and may show, for example, absolute values, percentages, or index numbers. Keep

Figure Example 4. A line graph as an alternative to a bar graph.

- Figure is simpler.
- More than one comparison at a time can be perceived.

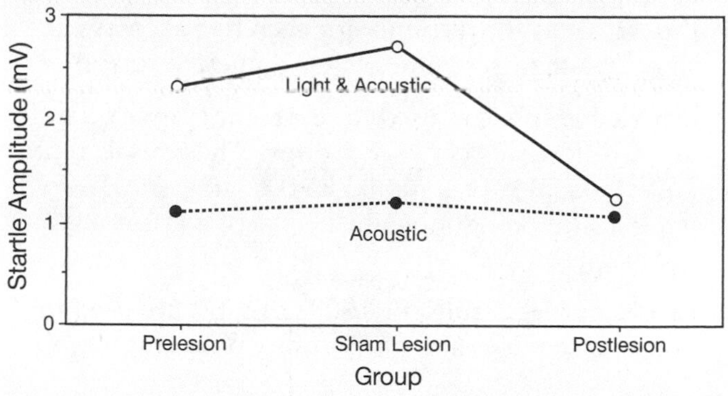

the lines clean and simple, and eliminate extraneous detail. The presentation of information on the horizontal (or x) and vertical (or y) axes should be orderly (e.g., small to large) and consistent (e.g., in comparable units of measurement).

- **Scatter plots** consist of single dots plotted to represent the values of single events on the two variables scaled on the abscissa and ordinates (see Figure Example 5). Meaningful clusters of dots imply correlations. For example, a cluster of dots along a diagonal implies a linear relationship, and if all the dots fall on a diagonal line, the coefficient of correlation is 1.00.

- **Line graphs** are used to show the relation between two quantitative variables. The independent variable is plotted on the horizontal axis, and the dependent variable is plotted on the vertical axis (see Figure Examples 1, 2, and 4). Grid marks on the axes demarcate units of measurement; scales on the axes can be linear (with equal numerical and visual increments, e.g., 25, 30, 35), logarithmic, or log-linear.

- **Bar graphs** are used when the independent variable is categorical (e.g., as with different experimental conditions; see Figure Example 3). Solid horizontal or vertical bars each represent one kind of datum. In a subdivided bar graph, each bar shows two or more divisions of data (note that comparison across bars is difficult for all but the first layer because they do not have a common baseline). Other bar graphs include multiple bar graphs (in which whole bars represent different single variables in one set of data) and sliding bar graphs (in which bars are split by a horizontal line that serves as the reference for each bar, such as to show less-than-zero and greater-than-zero relations).

- **Pictorial graphs** are used to represent simple quantitative differences between groups. All symbols representing equal values should be the same size. Keep in mind that if you double the height of a symbol, you quadruple its area.
- **Circle (or pie) graphs,** or 100% graphs, are used to show percentages and proportions. The number of

Figure Example 5. Sample scatter plot.[3]

- Solid circles represent data points.
- Zero point indicated on axes.
- Axis labels are in a legible typeface.

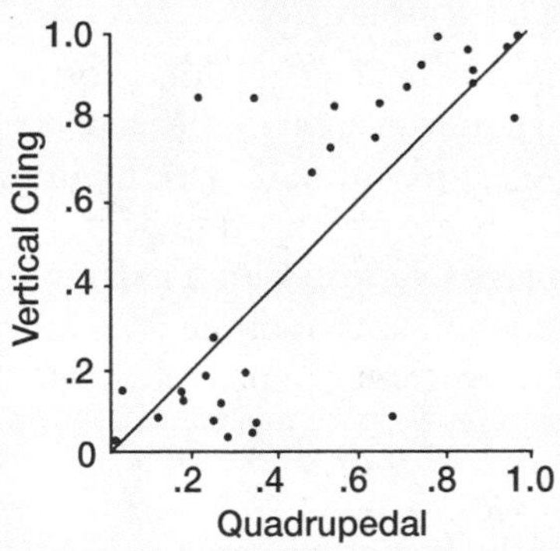

Figure X. Proportion of left-hand reaches by squirrel monkeys from horizontal quadrupedal and vertical cling postures in Experiment 1.

[List captions together on a separate page.]

[3]From "Postural Effects on Manual Reaching Laterality in Squirrel Monkeys (*Saimiri sciureus*) and Cotton-Top Tamarins (*Saguinus oedipus*)," by L. S. Roney and J. E. King, 1993, *Journal of Comparative Psychology, 107,* p. 382. Copyright 1993 by the American Psychological Association. Adapted with permission of the author.

items compared should be kept to five or fewer. Order the segments from large to small, beginning the largest segment at 12 o'clock. A good way to highlight differences is to shade the segments from light to dark, making the smallest segment the darkest. Use patterns of lines and dots to shade the segments.

Charts can describe the relations between parts of a group or object or the sequence of operations in a process; charts are usually boxes connected with lines. For example, organizational charts show the hierarchy in a group, flowcharts show the sequence of steps in a process, and schematics show components in a system. Figure Example 6 shows the elements of a theoretical model in a path analysis.

Figure Example 6. Sample chart (path model).[4]

- Names of variables are indicated with the variable symbols.
- Size of numbers is proportional to lettering, enabling complex figure to be placed in a small space on page.

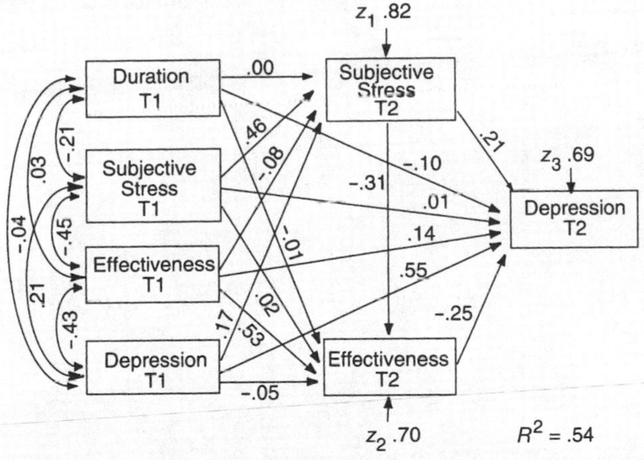

Figure X. Initial path-analytic model: Influence of caregiving duration, subjective caregiving stress, and subjective caregiving effectiveness on changes in depression.

[List captions together on a separate page.]

[4]From "Longitudinal Impact of Interhousehold Caregiving on Adult Children's Mental Health," by A. Townsend, L. Noelker, G. Deimling, and D. Bass, 1989, *Psychology and Aging, 4,* p. 395. Copyright 1989 by the American Psychological Association. Reprinted with permission of the author.

Dot maps can show population density, and **shaded maps** can show averages or percentages. In these cases, plotted data are superimposed on a map. Maps should always be prepared by a professional artist, who should clearly indicate the compass orientation (e.g., north–south) of the map, fully identify the map's location, and provide the scale to which the map is drawn. Use arrows to help readers focus on reference points.

Drawings are selective and give the author the flexibility to emphasize any aspect of an image or idea (see

***Figure Example 7.* Sample line drawing.**[5]

- Lines are simple; no extraneous detail.
- Type is legible.
- Arrangement of components of figure is compact.

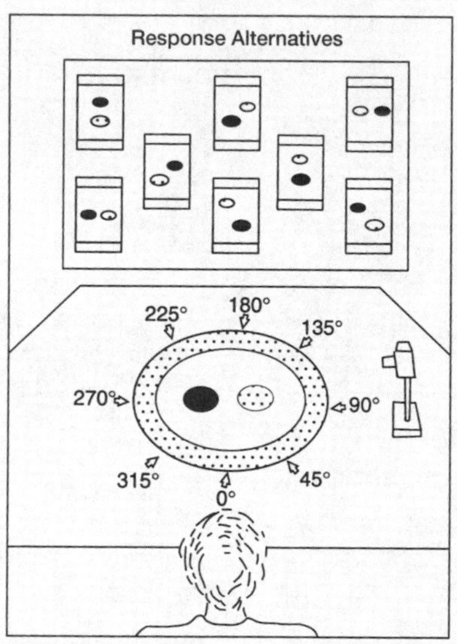

Figure X. The perspective-taking task. In the item depicted, the disks are in the horizontal orientation, the camera is at 90°, and the correct response is shown in the upper left corner of the response alternatives.

[List captions together on a separate page.]

[5]From "Understanding Person–Space–Map Relations: Cartographic and Developmental Perspectives," by L. S. Liben and R. M. Downs, 1993, *Developmental Psychology, 29,* p. 744. Copyright 1993 by the American Psychological Association. Reprinted with permission of the author.

Figure Example 7). They can be done from any of several views, for instance, a two-dimensional view of one side of an object or a view of an object rotated and tipped forward to show several sides at once. Drawings should be prepared by a professional artist and should use the least amount of detail necessary to convey the point.

Photographs have excellent eye appeal. They should be of professional quality and should be prepared with a background that produces the greatest amount of contrast. A photographer can highlight a particular aspect of the photograph by manipulating the camera angle or by choosing a particular type of lighting or film. (For more on photographs, see Using Photographs, pp. 113–115.)

Line Art Versus Halftone

Although there are many types of figures, usually only two printing processes are involved in reproducing them: line art processing and halftone processing. Line art is any material that will reproduce only in black and white, for example, type, lines, boxes, and dots; such material includes line graphs, charts, and bar graphs. Halftones are figures that have shades of gray—photographs and photomicrographs, for example (see Figure Example 8). Halftones require a special printing process, which makes them more expensive than line drawings to reproduce.

Overall Size and Proportion

When planning a figure, consider that

- All published figures must fit the dimensions of the journal in which your article will be published. Size your figures to fit within a single journal column unless multiple panels or fine detail require them to be the width of the journal page (see Table 6.1).
- Parallel figures or figures of equal importance should be of equal size; that is, they should be prepared according to the same scale.
- Combining like figures (e.g., two line graphs with identical axes) facilitates comparisons between them. For example, if each of two figures can be reduced to fit in a single column, place one above the other and treat them as one figure. Two line graphs with

identical axes might be combined horizontally and treated as one figure (see Figure Example 1).

- All elements of a figure, including plot points and subscripts, must be large enough to be legible (as a general rule, type should be no smaller than 8 point and no larger than 14 point).
- A figure legend, which is a key to symbols used in the figure, should be positioned within the borders of the figure (see Figure Examples 1 and 3). Place labels for parts of a figure as close as possible to the components being identified.

Figure Example 8. Sample photograph (halftone).[6]

- Cropped to omit extraneous detail and to fit in one column.
- Good contrast for reproduction.
- Panel label has good contrast to background.
- Scale bar included and labeled in 14-pt sans serif font.

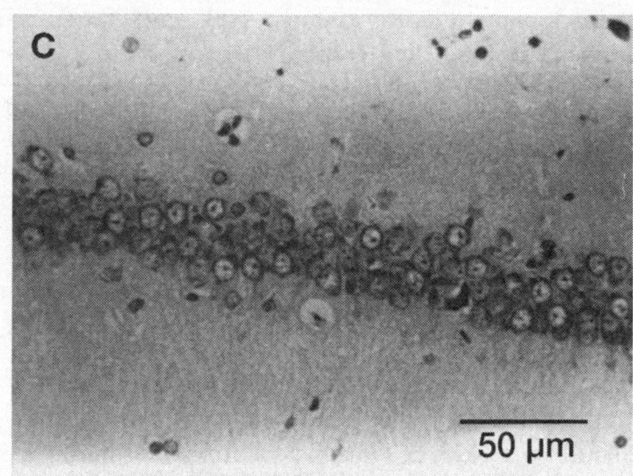

Figure X. Photomicrograph of part of the CA1 cell field from the control rat.

[List captions together on a separate page.]

[6]Panel from "Impaired Object Recognition Memory in Rats Following Ischemia-Induced Damage to the Hippocampus," by E. R. Wood, D. G. Mumby, J. P. J. Pinel, and A. G. Phillips, 1993, *Behavioral Neuroscience, 107,* p. 55. Copyright 1993 by the American Psychological Association. Reprinted with permission of the author.

Preparation of Figures

Figures may be mechanically produced or computer generated. Mechanical figure preparation usually should be done by graphic arts professionals because they have the technical skill to produce a figure that meets printing requirements. A graphic arts professional also may produce a figure with sophisticated computer software and hardware that typically are unavailable to authors.

Table 6.1. Sizing and Type Specifications for Figures for APA Journals

A. *Standard Figure Sizes*

APA journal dimension	Standard figure width: 1 column, Minimum	1 column, Maximum	2 columns, Minimum	2 columns, Maximum
Inches				
8¼ × 11	2	3¼	4¼	6⅞
6¾ × 10	2	2⅝	3⅝	5½
Centimeters				
21 × 28	5.0	8.45	10.60	17.50
17 × 25.4	5.0	6.70	9.30	14.00
Picas				
49.5 × 66	13	20	25	41.5
40.5 × 60	12	16	22	33

Note. Figures are sized to fit within the ranges shown. Simple line graphs and bar graphs will be reduced to fit into one column.

B. *Minimum and Maximum Type Sizes*

Minimum	Maximum
8 point	14 point
8 POINT	14 POINT
●○▲□	●○▲□

Note. For legibility, a sans serif typeface, such as Helvetica used above, is recommended. Other common sans serif typefaces are Futura, Univers, Geneva, and Optima. A combination of circles and triangles is recommended to distinguish curves on line graphs; the shapes remain distinctive after reduction, whereas circles and squares can look similar when reduced.

A glossy or high-quality laser print of any professional-quality figure is acceptable, however, whether created by a graphics specialist or generated by computer. If you generate figures by computer, resist the temptation to use special effects (e.g., three-dimensional effects in bar graphs and line graphs); although special effects may have eye-catching appeal and are popular in newsletters and magazines, they can distort data and distract the reader.

Whether prepared by graphic artist or author, drawn by hand or generated by a graphics software or statistical package, all figures must adhere to the following mechanical specifications to be acceptable for reproduction (camera ready).

Size and Proportion of Elements

Each element must be large enough and sharp enough to be legible (see Figure Example 9 for examples of good and poor proportions). The size of lettering should be no smaller than 8-point type and no larger than 14-point type (see Table 6.1 for examples of each). As a general guideline, plot symbols should be about the size of a lowercase letter of an average label within the figure. Also consider the weight (i.e., size, density) of each element in a figure in relation to that of every other element, making the most important elements the most prominent. For example, curves on line graphs and outlines of bars on bar graphs should be bolder than axis labels, which should be bolder than the axes and tick marks (Scientific Illustration Committee, 1988).

Shading

Drawings and graphs should be shaded in such a way that they can be reproduced as line art rather than as more expensive halftones. If different shadings are used to distinguish bars or segments of a graph, choose shadings that are distinct (e.g., the best option to distinguish two sets of bars is no shading [open] and black [solid]). Limit the number of different shadings used in one bar graph to two or three. If more are required, a table may be a better presentation of the data. Instead of using fine dot screens to create shades of gray in a bar graph, use a pattern of diagonal lines (hatching) or heavier dots (stippling). Diagonal lines produce the best effect; fine stippling and shading can "drop out," or disappear, when reproduced. If you use fine dot screens, be sure that different bars contrast with each other by at least 30% of gray tone (Scientific Illustration Committee, 1988). Computer-generated art will typically be produced as

Figure Example 9. Proportion examples.

Examples of poor (top) and good (bottom) proportions on originals (left) and their reductions at 80% (right). In the poor original, the type size varies from 4 to 16 points and is in an illegible "jagged," condensed style, which worsens with reduction; the shading, symbols, and lines improve slightly but are still too difficult to distinguish. The professional sans serif type in the good original holds up on reduction, as do the symbols and lines.[7]

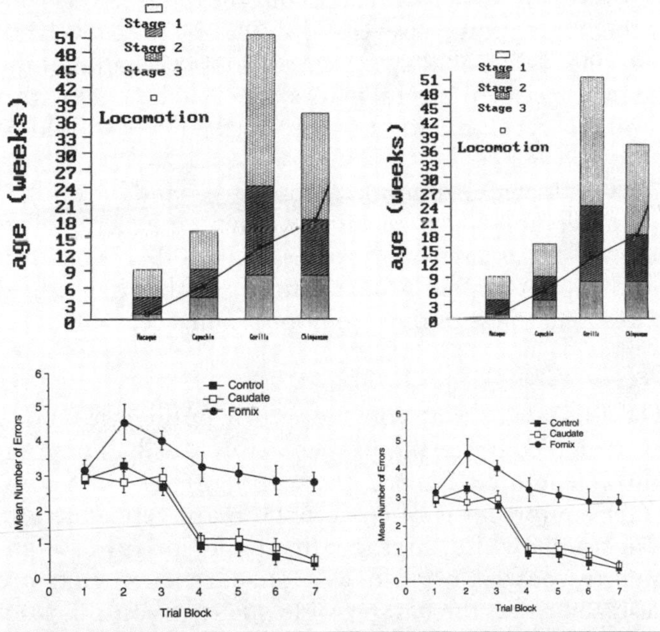

[7]Top panel used with permission from P. Poti and G. Spinozzi, whose revised art appeared in "Early Sensorimotor Development in Chimpanzees (*Pan troglodytes*)," 1994, *Journal of Comparative Psychology, 108,* p. 100. Bottom panel from "Double Dissociation of Fornix and Caudate Nucleus Lesions on Acquisition of Two Water Maze Tasks: Further Evidence for Multiple Memory Systems," by M. G. Packard and J. L. McGaugh, 1992, *Behavioral Neuroscience, 106,* p. 442. Copyright 1992 by the American Psychological Association. Adapted with permission of the author.

line art, as long as the image has been created through a digital process that places dots on the page.

Lettering

For either mechanical or computer-generated type, use a simple, sans serif typeface (such as Arial, Futura, or Helvetica) with enough space between letters to avoid crowding. Letters should be clear, sharp, and uniformly dark and should be as consistent a size as possible throughout the figure. Point size should vary by no more than 4 points; for example, if axis labels are 12 points, legend labels should be no smaller than 8 points, the minimum acceptable size of lettering.

Style of type also affects legibility: For example, type in boldface tends to thicken and become less legible when reproduced. Initial capitals and lowercase letters generally are easier to read than all capital letters, but if the figure requires several distinctions (i.e., levels) of lettering, occasional use of capitals is acceptable. If the figure consists of several panels, label each panel with a capital letter in the top left corner (the letter should be 14 point: A).

Typewritten or nonprofessional freehand lettering is not acceptable for publication. Computer-generated lettering that has a resolution of less than 300 dots per inch (such as dot-matrix printer output) or that has jagged edges, regardless of the resolution, is unacceptable.

Preparing the Final Print

The final print that you supply for publication must have high contrast and be reasonably sturdy. For computer-generated figures, the output from your computer equipment is often acceptable for reproduction. Use bright white, high-quality paper or other high-quality materials (such as transparencies) that are designed to get the best possible quality of output from your equipment. Check that the final print is sharp and free from smudges. If your computer-generated art includes shading, check the printout to make sure that all shading has an even tone so that “bald spots” do not occur in reproduction. (For additional information on submitting final prints, see Submitting Figures, pp. 116–117.)

Figure Example 10. Examples of unacceptable computer-generated art (left) and the revision (right).

Unacceptable

- Type is jagged and illegible.
- Curves are jagged.
- Axes labels are in all caps, and ordinate label reads verticially.
- Units of measure are not specified.

Acceptable

- Lettering is professional.
- Curves are smooth.
- Lettering is in caps and lowercase and runs parallel to axes.
- Units of measure are specified.
- Top border and right axis were removed.

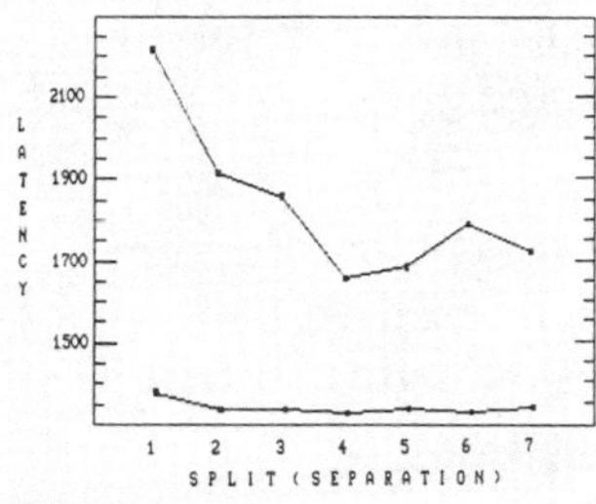

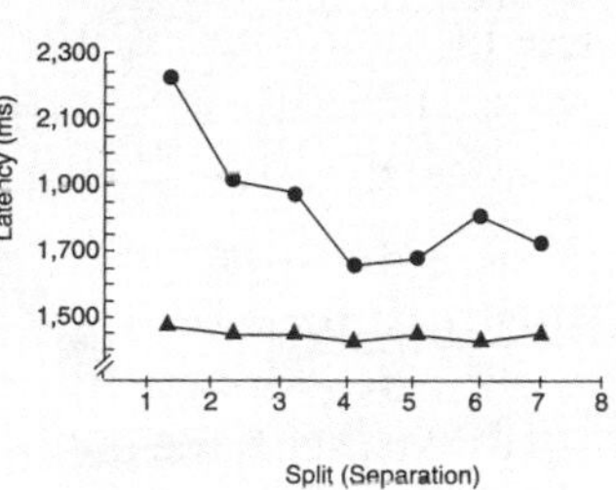

Submitting an Electronic Version of a Figure

APA is open to receiving digital art files, provided they meet the minimum requirements for printing. Authors also must provide a high-quality print as backup.

The graphic files with which printers are the most successful are TIFF or EPS files generated from a professional-level graphics program (such as Adobe Photoshop or Illustrator). The minimum requirements are as follows:

- *line art*—black-and-white (or bitmap), with a resolution of 1200 dots per inch;
- *halftones*—grayscale, with a resolution of 300 dots per inch; and
- *combination halftones* (halftones with superimposed labels or lettering)—grayscale, with a resolution of 600 dots per inch.

Files created in standard office software (e.g., for word processing, spreadsheet functions, or presentations) cannot be used for printing, primarily because the resolution of the files is too low. Files created in presentation software are unacceptable because the maximum resolution is only 72 dots per inch.

Creating Graphs

Follow these guidelines in creating a graph mechanically or with a computer. Computer software that generates graphs will often handle most of these steps automatically. Nevertheless, you should examine the resulting graph to ensure that it follows these guidelines and make any needed adjustments.

- Use bright white paper.
- Use medium lines for the vertical and horizontal axes. The best aspect ratio of the graph may depend on the data.
- Choose the appropriate grid scale. Consider the range and scale separation to be used on both axes and the overall dimensions of the figure so that plotted curves span the entire illustration.
- In line graphs, a change in the proportionate sizes of the x units to the y units changes the slant of the line. Thus, for example, disproportionately large units on the vertical axis will exaggerate differences. Be sure the curve or slant of the line accurately reflects the data.
- Indicate units of measurement by placing tick marks on each axis at the appropriate intervals. Use equal increments of space between tick marks on linear scales.
- If the units of measurement on the axes do not begin at zero, break the axes with a double slash.
- Clearly label each axis with both the quantity measured and the units in which the quantity is measured. Carry numerical labels for axis intervals to the same number of decimal places.
- Position the axis label parallel to its axis. Do not stack letters so that the label reads vertically; do not

place a label perpendicular to the vertical (y) axis unless it is very short (i.e., two words or a maximum of 10 characters). The numbering and lettering of grid points should be horizontal on both axes.

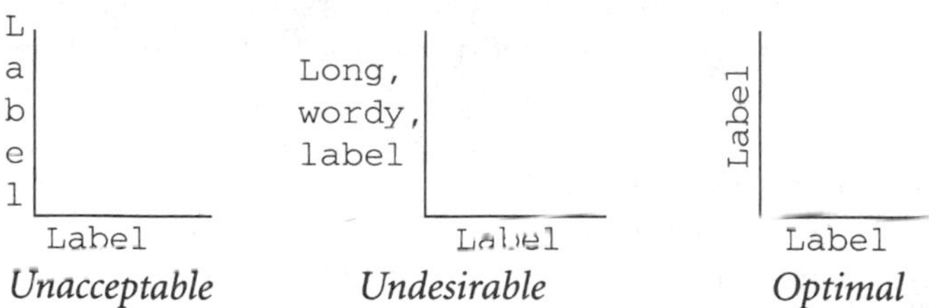

Unacceptable *Undesirable* *Optimal*

- Use legibility as a guide in determining the number of curves to place on a figure—usually no more than four curves per graph. Allow adequate space between and within curves, remembering that the figure may need to be reduced.
- Use distinct, simple geometric forms for plot points; good choices are open and solid circles and triangles. Combinations of squares and circles or squares and diamonds are not recommended because they can be difficult to differentiate if the art is reduced, as can open symbols with dots inside (e.g., ⊙)

Using Photographs

Because reproduction softens contrast and detail in photographs, starting with rich contrast and sharp prints is important. The camera view and the lighting should highlight the subject and provide high contrast; a light or dark background can provide even more contrast.

Photographs must be of professional quality and on black-and-white film. Do not submit color prints because the transition from color to black and white for reproduction is unpredictable and usually inaccurate in tone. Have a color negative, slide, or print developed as a black-and-white print before submitting it for publication. (If you intend to have a photograph printed in color, be sure to consult your publisher or the publication's instructions to authors.)

Photographs usually benefit from cropping (i.e., eliminating what is not to be reproduced). Cropping recomposes the photograph, eliminates extraneous detail, and recenters the image. Cropping can also remove blemishes.

To prepare for cropping a photograph, first determine the ideal area to be reproduced, that is, the part of the photograph that will appear on the printed page. The area to be reproduced need not be the same shape as the larger photograph, but the edges should be straight lines at right angles to each other.

Next, mark the area to be reproduced. One way to indicate the area is to outline it on a piece of acetate or tissue paper covering the photograph. Write lightly with a felt-tipped pen on tissue overlays. Never write directly on the face of the photograph.

Finally, have a print made of the outlined area of the photograph, and submit the new print with the manuscript.

If you group photographs for purposes of comparison or to save space, butt the photographs right next to each other. The printer can insert a thin white or black line between the photographs to separate them. Some printers prefer unmounted photographs for compatibility with reproduction equipment; be sure to consult the publication's instructions to authors for this information.

Photomicrographs are produced with specialized equipment. Photomicrographs should be submitted so that they can be reproduced at their exact size for optimal print quality. Therefore, be sure to find out which dimensions are acceptable for the journal to which you are submitting your manuscript (for APA journals, see Table 6.1). If you mark on a tissue or acetate overlay the most important areas of the photomicrograph, the printer can pay particular attention to them when making the halftone. Indicate the degree of magnification by including a scale line on the photograph. Also, indicate in the figure caption the type of staining materials and any unusual lighting used.

If you photograph a person, get a signed release from that person to use the photograph. If you use a photograph from another source, try to obtain the original photograph because photographs of photographs do not print clearly. Obtain written permission for reuse (in both print and electronic form) from the copyright holder, and acknowledge the author and the copyright holder in the figure caption (see Tables From Another Source, p. 95).

Identifying and Citing Figures

Number all figures consecutively with arabic numerals throughout an article in the order in which they are first mentioned in text (i.e., Figure 1, Figure 2). This number should appear as close to the top right edge of the figure print as possible, *outside* of the image area. If the image area takes up the entire print, write the number on the back of the figure instead. Also on the back of the print, write the article's short title and the word *TOP* to designate the top of the figure.

In the text, refer to figures by their numbers:

as shown in Figure 2, the relationships are

data are related (see Figure 5)

Never write "the figure above" (or below) or "the figure on page 12," because the position and page number of a figure cannot be determined until the typesetter lays out the pages.

Figure Legends and Captions

In APA journals, a legend explains the symbols used in the figure; it is placed within and photographed as part of the figure. A caption is a concise explanation of the figure; it is typeset and placed below the figure.

On the final print, make certain that the symbols, abbreviations, and terminology in the caption and legend agree with the symbols, abbreviations, and terminology in the figure, in other figures in the article, and in the text. When preparing the final version for production and again when proofing the typeset article, compare the caption with the figure; proofread all lettering, and make sure no labels are missing.

Legends

The legend is an integral part of the figure; therefore, it should have the same kind and proportion of lettering that appear in the rest of the figure. Because it is scanned as part of the figure, the legend must appear on the final print, preferably within the axis area (if any). Capitalize major words in the legend.

Captions

The caption serves both as an explanation of the figure and as a figure title; therefore, the artwork should not include a title. The caption should be a brief but descriptive phrase. Compare the following captions.

Too brief:

> *Figure 3.* Fixation duration.

Sufficiently descriptive:

> *Figure 3.* Fixation duration as a function of the delay between the beginning of eye fixation and the onset of the stimulus in Experiment 1.

After the descriptive phrase, add any information needed to clarify the figure: A reader should not have to refer to the text to decipher the figure's message. Always explain units of measurement, symbols, and abbreviations that are not included in the legend. If your graph includes error bars, explain whether they represent standard deviations, standard errors, confidence limits, or ranges; it is also helpful to define the sample sizes used (see Figure Example 1). If statistically significant values are marked in the figure, explain the probability in the caption (follow the same system used for table notes; see Notes to a Table, pp. 91–94).

Because the caption is typeset and placed outside the figure, type all figure captions, with their numbers, double-spaced starting on a separate sheet.

If you reproduced or adapted your figure from a copyrighted source, you must obtain written permission for print and electronic reuse from the copyright holder and give credit in the figure caption to the original author and copyright holder. Use the wording shown in Tables From Another Source (p. 95), and place this notice at the end of the caption.

Submitting Figures

With the original submitted manuscript, paper copies of figures are acceptable. Glossy or final prints must be prepared before the manuscript is accepted for publication. Final figures must be photographed and submitted as 8 × 10 in. (20 × 25 cm) glossy prints or submitted as final prints on bright white paper. Computer-generated figures should be on 8½ × 11 in. (22 × 28 cm) high-quality, bright white paper or other material that produces a sharp image and high contrast. If it is necessary to submit smaller prints, remount them on 8½ × 11 in. (22 × 28 cm) paper.

To reproduce the figure, the printer scans the glossy or final print to create a digital image file. Flaws in the glossy or final print will appear in the published figure. Therefore, do not attach anything to the print with staples or paper clips, and avoid pressing down on the print when you write the identification information on the back. Protect the figure by putting a piece of tissue paper over it. Place the prints between pieces of cardboard to protect them.

Figure Checklist

- Is the figure necessary?
- Is the figure simple, clean, and free of extraneous detail?
- Are the data plotted accurately?
- Is the grid scale correctly proportioned?
- Is the lettering large and dark enough to read? Is the lettering compatible in size with the rest of the figure? (Freehand, typewritten, or jagged computer-generated lettering is not acceptable.)
- Are parallel figures or equally important figures prepared according to the same scale?
- Are terms spelled correctly?
- Are all abbreviations and symbols explained in a figure legend or figure caption? Are the symbols, abbreviations, and terminology in the figure consistent with those in the figure caption? In other figures? In the text?
- Are digital files in TIFF format at the appropriate resolution and accompanied by a high-quality laser printout?
- Are all figure captions typed together on a separate page?

- Are the figures numbered consecutively with arabic numerals?
- Are all figures mentioned in the text?
- Is each figure an 8 × 10 in. (20 × 25 cm) glossy print or photostat or an 8½ × 11 in. (22 × 28 cm) final print?
- Are all figures identified lightly in pencil or felt-tip pen by figure number (on the front or back) and short article title (on the back)?
- Is TOP written on the back of figures to show orientation?
- Is written permission for print and electronic reuse enclosed for figures that are being reproduced or adapted from another source? Is proper credit given in the figure caption?

7 Footnotes and Appendixes

This chapter describes the use of footnotes and appendixes. Notes may be substantive or explanatory or may identify sources, according to where they are used and what information needs to be conveyed. The first section defines the kinds of notes in APA journals, including footnotes in text, notes to tables, and author notes. The purpose of appendixes, how to identify and cite them in text, tables as appendixes, as well as tests and questionnaires are then discussed in the second section.

Footnotes

Footnotes in Text

Footnotes in text are of two kinds: content footnotes and copyright permission footnotes.

Content footnotes supplement or amplify substantive information in the text; they should not include complicated, irrelevant, or nonessential information. Because they are distracting to readers and expensive to include in printed material, such footnotes should be included only if they strengthen the discussion. A content footnote should convey just one idea; if you find yourself creating paragraphs or displaying equations as you are writing a footnote, then the main text or an appendix probably would be a more suitable place to present your information (see Appendixes, pp. 122–124 for more information on appendixes). Another alternative to consider is to indicate in a short footnote that the material is available from the author. In most cases, an author integrates an article best by presenting important information in the text, not in a footnote.

Copyright permission footnotes acknowledge the source of quotations (see Permission to Quote, pp.

129–130). Use the suggested wording for reprinted tables or figures (see Tables From Another Source, p. 95). All other kinds of reference citations, including legal citations and citations to material of limited availability, should appear in the reference list (see chap. 8).

Number content and copyright permission footnotes consecutively throughout an article with superscript arabic numerals. Type these footnotes on a separate page. Subsequent references to a footnote are by parenthetical note:

the same results (see Footnote 3)

Notes to Tables

Table notes, which are placed below the bottom rule of a table, explain the table data or provide additional information (see Notes to a Table, pp. 91–94). They also acknowledge the source of a table if the table is reprinted (see Tables From Another Source, p. 95 for suggested wording).

Author Note

An author note appears with each printed article to identify each author's departmental affiliation, provide acknowledgments, state any disclaimers or perceived conflict of interest, and provide a point of contact for the interested reader. Notes should be arranged as follows.

First Paragraph: Complete Departmental Affiliation. Identify departmental affiliations at the time of the study for all authors. Format as follows: name of the author as it appears in the byline, comma, department name, comma, university or institution name, semicolon, next author name, and so on, and end with a period. Because the order of authorship is shown in the byline, the copy editor may edit the departmental affiliations paragraph to conserve space (e.g., if some authors are in the same departments). If an author is not affiliated with an institution, provide the city and state (provide city and country for authors whose affiliations are outside of the United States, and include province for authors in Canada or Australia). No academic degrees should be given, and state names should be spelled out.

Second Paragraph: Changes of Affiliation (if any). Identify any changes in author affiliation subsequent to the time of the study. Use the following wording: [author's name] is now at [affiliation].

Third Paragraph: Acknowledgments. Identify grants or other financial support (and the source, if appropriate) for your study; do not precede grant numbers by No. or #. Next, acknowledge colleagues who assisted you in conducting the study or critiquing your manuscript. Do not acknowledge the persons routinely involved in the review and acceptance of manuscripts—peer reviewers or editors, associate editors, and consulting editors of the journal in which the article is to appear. (If you would like to acknowledge a specific idea raised by a reviewer, do so in the text where the idea is discussed.) In this paragraph you may also explain any special agreements concerning authorship, such as if you and your colleagues contributed equally to the study. You may end this paragraph with thanks for personal assistance, such as in manuscript preparation.

This paragraph is the appropriate place to disclose any special circumstances; explain them before providing the routine information described in the previous paragraph. For example, if your paper is based on an earlier study (e.g., a longitudinal study), a doctoral dissertation, or a paper presented at a meeting, state that information in this paragraph. Also, acknowledge the publication of related reports (e.g., reports on the same database). If any relationships may be perceived as a conflict of interest (e.g., if you own stock in a company that manufactures a drug used in your study), explain them here. If your employer or granting organization requires a disclaimer stating, for example, that the research reported does not reflect the views of that organization, such a statement is included in this paragraph.

Fourth Paragraph: Point of Contact (Mailing Address, E-Mail). Provide a complete mailing address for correspondence (see the example that follows for appropriate wording); names of states should be written out, not abbreviated, for ease of international mailing. You may end this paragraph with an e-mail address.

> John Doe, Department of Psychology, University of Illinois at Urbana–Champaign; Jane Smith, Department of Educational Psychology, University of Chicago.

> Jane Smith is now at Department of Psychology and Family Studies, University of California, San Diego.
>
> This research was supported in part by grants from the National Institute on Aging and from the John D. and Catherine T. MacArthur Foundation.
>
> Correspondence concerning this article should be addressed to John Doe, Department of Psychology, University of Illinois, Champaign, Illinois 61820. E-mail: jdoe@uiuc.edu

Unlike content footnotes, the author note is not numbered; the note should be typed on a page separate from the main text and from any content footnotes. If the manuscript is to receive a masked review, type the author note on the title page.

Appendixes

An appendix serves two purposes: It allows the author to provide the reader with detailed information that would be distracting to read in the main body of the article, and it enables production staff to be more flexible with rules of style and layout. If you submit a list of words as a table, for example, the copy editor may (a) request column and stub headings to make the list fit APA Style for tables or (b) suggest placing the list in an appendix.

Common kinds of appendixes include a mathematical proof, a large table, lists of words, a sample of a questionnaire or other survey instrument used in the research, and a computer program. A paper may include more than one appendix.

Identifying and Citing Appendixes

If your paper has only one appendix, label it Appendix; if your paper has more than one appendix, label each one with a capital letter (Appendix A, Appendix B, etc.) in the order in which it is mentioned in the main text. Each appendix must have a title. In the text, refer to appendixes by their labels:

> produced the same results for both studies (see Appendixes A and B for complete proofs).

Body and Headings

Like the main text, an appendix may include headings and subheadings. (To determine levels of heading within an appendix, treat the appendix separate from the main text: For example, the main text may have four levels of heading, but if the appendix has only two levels of heading, treat the appendix as if it were a two-level paper; see Selecting the Levels of Heading, pp. 28–29.) Like the main text, an appendix also may include tables, figures, and displayed equations. Number each appendix table and figure, and number displayed equations if necessary for later reference; precede the number with the letter of the appendix in which it is included (e.g., Table A1). In a sole appendix, which is not labeled with a letter, precede all tables, figures, and equation numbers with the letter *A* to distinguish them from those of the main text. The same rules for citation that apply to the main text apply to appendixes: All appendix tables and figures must be cited within the appendix and numbered in order of citation.

Tables as Appendixes

If one table constitutes an entire appendix, the centered appendix label and title serve in lieu of a table number and title. Generally, treat multiple tables as separate appendixes. If multiple tables (but no text) are combined into one appendix, number the tables.

Tests and Questionnaires

If you would like to publish a new test or questionnaire in an APA journal, APA will own the copyright. (Authors who wish to retain copyright to a measure they believe might have commercial value can do so by indicating "copyright [year] by [author name].")

If you want to reprint another author's test or questionnaire, you must determine whether permission is required from the copyright holder, obtain permission for print and electronic reuse when it is required, and give full credit in your article to the copyright holder. When permission is required, send the permission letter when transmitting your accepted manuscript for publication.

Cautionary Note: A number of commercial instruments—for example, intelligence tests and projective measures—are highly protected. Permission is required, and may be denied, to republish even one item from such instruments. You should seek permission from the copyright holder before submission of papers containing such items. Publishers will require written evidence that such permission has been obtained. If there is any question concerning the copyright protection of such items, permission should be requested early in the process of writing the paper.

8 Quotations, Reference Citations in Text, and Reference List

This chapter illustrates the application of APA Style to direct quotation of a source, reference citations in text, and the reference list. The first section discusses important aspects of quoting from sources, such as accuracy, changes from a source requiring and not requiring explanation, citation of sources, and permission to quote. In the second section, the correct format for various types of in-text citations is outlined, including one work by multiple authors, groups as authors, and works with no author, among others. The last section introduces APA reference style and describes the main elements of common types of references.

Quotations

Quotation of Sources

Material directly quoted from another author's work or from one's own previously published work, material duplicated from a test item, and verbatim instructions to participants should be reproduced word for word. Incorporate a short quotation (fewer than 40 words) into text, and enclose the quotation with double quotation marks. (See Quotation Marks, pp. 34–35, for other uses of double quotation marks.)

Display a quotation of 40 or more words in a freestanding block of typewritten lines, and omit the quotation marks. Start such a *block quotation* on a new line, and indent the block about ½ in. (1.3 cm, or five spaces) from the left margin (in the same position as a new paragraph). If there are additional paragraphs within the quotation, indent the first line of each an additional ½ in. The entire quotation should be double-spaced.

The following examples illustrate the application of APA Style to direct quotation of a source. When quoting, always provide the author, year, and specific page citation in the text, and include a complete reference in the reference list.

Quotation 1:

She stated, "The 'placebo effect' . . . disappeared when behaviors were studied in this manner" (Miele, 1993, p. 276), but she did not clarify which behaviors were studied.

Quotation 2:

Miele (1993) found that "the 'placebo effect,' which had been verified in previous studies, disappeared when [only the first group's] behaviors were studied in this manner" (p. 276).

Quotation 3:

Miele (1993) found the following:

> The "placebo effect," which had been verified in previous studies, disappeared when behaviors were studied in this manner. Furthermore, the behaviors *were never exhibited again* [italics added], even when reel [*sic*] drugs were administered. Earlier studies (e.g., Abdullah, 1984; Fox, 1979) were clearly premature in attributing the results to a placebo effect. (p. 276)

Accuracy

Direct quotations must be accurate. Except as noted in Changes From the Source Requiring No Explanation (p. 127) and Changes From the Source Requiring Explanation (pp. 127–128), the quotation must follow the wording, spelling, and interior punctuation of the original source, even if the source is incorrect.

If any incorrect spelling, punctuation, or grammar in the source might confuse readers, insert the word *sic*, italicized and bracketed, immediately after the error in the quotation. (See Quotation 3 in the previous section, and see Changes From the Source Requiring Explanation, p. 127, for the use of brackets.) Always check the manuscript copy against the source to ensure that there are no discrepancies.

Double or Single Quotation Marks

In Text. Use double quotation marks to enclose quotations in text. Use single quotation marks within double quotation marks to set off material that in the original source was enclosed in double quotation marks (see the previous section, Quotation 2).

In Block Quotations (any quotations of 40 or more words). Do not use quotation marks to enclose block quotations. Do use double quotation marks to enclose any quoted material within a block quotation (see the previous section, Quotation 3).

With Other Punctuation. Place periods and commas within closing single or double quotation marks. Place other punctuation marks inside quotation marks only when they are part of the quoted material.

Changes From the Source Requiring No Explanation

The first letter of the first word in a quotation may be changed to an uppercase or a lowercase letter. The punctuation mark at the end of a sentence may be changed to fit the syntax. Single quotation marks may be changed to double quotation marks and vice versa (see preceding section). Any other changes (e.g., italicizing words for emphasis or omitting words) must be explicitly indicated (see next section).

Changes From the Source Requiring Explanation

Omitting Material. Use three spaced ellipsis points (. . .) within a sentence to indicate that you have omitted material from the original source (see Quotation of Sources, Quotation 1, p. 126). Use four points to indicate any omission between two sentences. The first point indicates the period at the end of the first sentence quoted, and the three spaced ellipsis points follow. Do not use ellipsis points at the beginning or end of any quotation unless, to prevent misinterpretation, you need to emphasize that the quotation begins or ends in midsentence.

Inserting Material. Use brackets, not parentheses, to enclose material (additions or explanations) inserted in a quotation by some person other than the original author (see Quotation of Sources, Quotation 2, p. 126).

Adding Emphasis. If you want to emphasize a word or words in a quotation, italicize the word or words. Immediately after the italicized words, insert within brackets the words *italics added*, that is, [italics added] (see Quotation of Sources, Quotation 3, p. 126).

Citation of Sources

Whether paraphrasing or quoting an author directly, you must credit the source. For a direct quotation in the text, the information provided will vary depending on whether your source was in print or electronic form. When citing print sources, give the author, year, and page number in parentheses.

Many electronic sources do not provide page numbers (unless they are PDF reproductions of printed material). If paragraph numbers are visible, use them in place of page numbers. Use the ¶ symbol or the abbreviation para.

> As Myers (2000, ¶ 5) aptly phrased it, "positive emotions are both an end—better to live fulfilled, with joy [and other positive emotions]—and a means to a more caring and healthy society."

If there are headings in the document and neither paragraph nor page numbers are visible, cite the heading and the number of the ¶ following it to direct the reader to the location of the quoted material.

> "The current system of managed care and the current approach to defining empirically supported treatments are shortsighted" (Beutler, 2000, Conclusion section, para. 1)

In some cases, it may be necessary to omit a location reference altogether, such as when no page or paragraph numbers are visible and headings either are not provided or would prove unwieldy or confusing. In documents accessed with a Web browser, readers will be able to search for the quoted material.

When paraphrasing or referring to an idea contained in another work, authors are not required to provide a location reference (e.g., a page or paragraph number). Nevertheless, authors are encouraged to do so, especially when it would help an interested reader locate the relevant passage in a long or complex text.

Punctuation around source citations will differ depending on where the quotation or paraphrased material falls within a sentence or the text.

In Midsentence. End the passage with quotation marks, cite the source in parentheses immediately after the quotation marks, and continue the sentence. Use no other punctuation unless the meaning of the sentence requires such punctuation (see Quotation of Sources, Quotation 1, p. 126).

At the End of a Sentence. Close the quoted passage with quotation marks, cite the source in parentheses immediately after the quotation marks, and end with the period or other punctuation outside the final parenthesis (see Quotation of Sources, Quotation 2, p. 126).

At the End of a Block Quote. Cite the quoted source in parentheses after the final punctuation mark (see Quotation of Sources, Quotation 3, p. 126).

Citations Within Quotations

Do not omit citations embedded within the original material you are quoting. The works cited need not be included in the list of references (unless you happen to cite them elsewhere in your paper).

Permission to Quote

Any direct quotation, regardless of length, must be accompanied by a reference citation that, if at all possible, includes a page number. (For the form of the citation of a source, see Reference Citations in Text, pp. 131–137.) If you quote at length from a copyrighted work in material you intend to publish, you usually also need written permission from the owner of the copyright. Requirements for obtaining permission to quote copyrighted material vary from one copyright owner to another; for example, APA policy permits use of up to 500 words of APA-copyrighted journal text without explicit permission. It is the author's responsibility to determine whether permission is required from the copyright owner and to obtain it for both print and electronic reuse when required. APA cannot publish previously copyrighted material that exceeds the copyright holder's determination of "fair use" without permission.

If you must obtain written permission from the copyright owner, append a footnote to the quoted material with a superscript number, and in the footnote, acknowledge permission from the owner of the copyright. Format the footnote like the permission footnotes used for tables and figures (see Tables From Another Source, p. 95), but substitute the indented superscript number for the word *Note*. Place the footnote number at the end of the quotation, after any punctuation. Enclose a copy of the letter of permission with the final version of the manuscript.

The "Ethical Principles of Psychologists and Code of Conduct" (APA, 2002) contain a number of principles that address the reporting and publishing of scientific data.

Plagiarism (Principle 8.11)

Psychologists do not claim the words and ideas of another as their own; they give credit where credit is due. Quotation marks should be used to indicate the exact words of another. *Each time* you paraphrase another author (i.e., summarize a passage or rearrange the order of a sentence and change some of the words), you will need to credit the source in the text. The following paragraph is an example of how one might appropriately paraphrase some of the foregoing material in this section:

> As stated in the fifth edition of the *Publication Manual of the American Psychological Association*, the ethical principles of scientific publication are designed to ensure the integrity of scientific knowledge and to protect the intellectual property rights of others. As the *Publication Manual* explains, authors are expected to correct the record if they discover errors in their publications; they are also expected to give credit to others for their prior work when it is quoted or paraphrased.

The key element of this principle is that an author does not present the work of another as if it were his or her own work. This can extend to ideas as well as written words. If an author models a study after one done by someone else, the originating author should be given credit. If the rationale for a study was suggested in the Discussion section of someone else's article, that person should be given credit. Given the free exchange of ideas, which is very important to the health of psychology, an author may not know where an idea for a study originated. If the author does know, however, the author should acknowledge the source; this includes personal communications. (Instructions on referencing publications and personal communications are described next.)

Reference Citations in Text

Document your study throughout the text by citing by author and date the works you used in your research. This style of citation briefly identifies the source for readers and enables them to locate the source of information in the alphabetical reference list at the end of the article. (See pp. 138–149, on the preparation of the reference list.)

Agreement of Text and Reference List

References cited in text must appear in the reference list; conversely, each entry in the reference list must be cited in text. The author must make certain that each source referenced appears in both places and that the text citation and reference list entry are identical in spelling and year.

One Work by One Author

APA journals use the author–date method of citation; that is, the surname of the author (do not include suffixes such as *Jr.*) and the year of publication are inserted in the text at the appropriate point:

Walker (2000) compared reaction times

In a recent study of reaction times (Walker, 2000)

If the name of the author appears as part of the narrative, as in the first example, cite only the year of publication in parentheses. Otherwise, place both the name and the year, separated by a comma, in parentheses (as in the second example). Even if the reference includes month and year, include only the year in the text citation. In the rare case in which both the year and the author are given as part of the textual discussion, do not add parenthetical information:

In 2000 Walker compared reaction times

Within a paragraph, you need not include the year in subsequent references to a study as long as the study cannot be confused with other studies cited in the article:

In a recent study of reaction times, Walker (2000) described the method. . . . Walker also found

One Work by Multiple Authors

When a work has two authors, always cite both names every time the reference occurs in text.

When a work has three, four, or five authors, cite all authors the first time the reference occurs; in subsequent citations, include only the surname of the first author followed by et al. (not italicized and with a period after "al") and the year if it is the first citation of the reference within a paragraph:

Wasserstein, Zappulla, Rosen, Gerstman, and Rock (1994) found [Use as first citation in text.]

Wasserstein et al. (1994) found [Use as subsequent first citation per paragraph thereafter.]

Wasserstein et al. found [Omit year from subsequent citations after first citation within a paragraph.]

Exception: If two references with the same year shorten to the same form (e.g., both Bradley, Ramirez, & Soo, 1994, and Bradley, Soo, Ramirez, & Brown, 1994, shorten to Bradley et al., 1994), cite the surnames of the first authors and of as many of the subsequent authors as necessary to distinguish the two references, followed by a comma and et al.

Bradley, Ramirez, and Soo (1994) and Bradley, Soo, et al. (1994)

When a work has six or more authors, cite only the surname of the first author followed by et al. (not italicized and with a period after "al") and the year for the first and subsequent citations. (In the reference list, however, because et al. translates to "and others," a decision was made to spell out six authors and seven authors and to use et al. after the sixth author for eight or more authors.)

If two references with six or more authors shorten to the same form, cite the surnames of the first authors and of as many of the subsequent authors as necessary to distinguish the two references, followed by a comma and et al. For example, suppose you have entries for the following references:

Kosslyn, Koenig, Barrett, Cave, Tang, and Gabrieli (1996)

Kosslyn, Koenig, Gabrieli, Tang, Marsolek, and Daly (1996)

In text you would cite them, respectively, as

Kosslyn, Koenig, Barrett, et al. (1996) and Kosslyn, Koenig, Gabrieli, et al. (1996)

Join the names in a multiple-author citation in running text by the word *and*. In parenthetical material, in tables and captions, and in the reference list, join the names by an ampersand (&):

as Nightlinger and Littlewood (1993) demonstrated

as has been shown (Jöreskog & Sörbom, 1989)

Groups as Authors

The names of groups that serve as authors (e.g., corporations, associations, government agencies, and study groups) are usually spelled out each time they appear in a text citation. The names of some group authors (e.g., associations, government agencies) are spelled out in the first citation and abbreviated thereafter. In deciding whether to abbreviate the name of a group author, use the general rule that you need to give enough information in the text citation for the reader to locate the entry in the reference list without difficulty. If the name is long and cumbersome and if the abbreviation is familiar or readily understandable, you may abbreviate the name in the second and subsequent citations. If the name is short or if the abbreviation would not be readily understandable, write out the name each time it occurs.

For example, the following group author is readily identified by its abbreviation:

Entry in reference list:

National Institute of Mental Health. (1999).

First text citation:

(National Institute of Mental Health [NIMH], 1999)

Subsequent text citations:

(NIMH, 1999)

The name of the following group author should be written out in full:

Entry in reference list:

University of Pittsburgh. (1993).

All text citations:

(University of Pittsburgh, 1993)

Works With No Author (Including Legal Materials) or With an Anonymous Author

When a work has no author, cite in text the first few words of the reference list entry (usually the title) and the year. Use double quotation marks around the title of an article or chapter, and italicize the title of a periodical, book, brochure, or report:

on free care ("Study Finds," 1982)

the book *College Bound Seniors* (1979)

Treat references to legal materials like references to works with no author; that is, in text, cite materials such as court cases, statutes, and legislation by the first few words of the reference and the year.

When a work's author is designated as "Anonymous," cite in text the word *Anonymous* followed by a comma and the date:

(Anonymous, 1998)

In the reference list, an anonymous work is alphabetized by the word *Anonymous* (see Order of References in the Reference List, pp. 139–141).

Authors With the Same Surname

If a reference list includes publications by two or more primary authors with the same surname, include the first author's initials in all text citations, even if the year of publication differs. Initials help the reader to avoid confusion within the text and to locate the entry in the list of references (see Order of References in the Reference List, pp. 139–141):

R. D. Luce (1959) and P. A. Luce (1986) also found

J. M. Goldberg and Neff (1961) and M. E. Goldberg and Wurtz (1972) studied

Two or More Works Within the Same Parentheses

Order the citations of two or more works within the same parentheses in the same order in which they appear in the reference list (see Order of References in the Reference List, pp. 139–141), according to the following guidelines.

Arrange two or more works by the same authors (in the same order) by year of publication. Place in-press citations last. Give the authors' surnames once; for each subsequent work, give only the date.

Past research (Edeline & Weinberger, 1991, 1993)

Past research (Gogel, 1984, 1990, in press)

Identify works by the same author (or by the same two or more authors in the same order) with the same publication date by the suffixes a, b, c, and so forth after the year; repeat the year. The suffixes are assigned in the reference list, where these kinds of references are ordered alphabetically by title (of the article, chapter, or complete work).

Several studies (Johnson, 1991a, 1991b, 1991c; Singh, 1983, in press-a, in press-b)

List two or more works by different authors who are cited within the same parentheses in alphabetical order by the first author's surname. Separate the citations with semicolons:

Several studies (Balda, 1980; Kamil, 1988; Pepperberg & Funk, 1990)

Exception: You may separate a major citation from other citations within parentheses by inserting a phrase, such as see also, before the first of the remaining citations, which should be in alphabetical order:

(Minor, 2001; see also Adams, 1999; Storandt, 1997)

Classical Works

When a work has no date of publication (see Publication Date, pp. 144–145), cite in text the author's name, followed by a comma and n.d. for "no date." When a date of publication is inapplicable, such as for some very old works, cite the year of the translation you used, preceded by trans., or the year of the version you used, followed by version. When you know the original date of publication, include this in the citation.

(Aristotle, trans. 1931)

James (1890/1983)

Reference entries are not required for major classical works, such as ancient Greek and Roman works and the Bible; simply identify in the first citation in the text the version you used. Parts of classical works (e.g., books, chapters, verses, lines, cantos) are numbered systematically across all editions, so use these numbers instead of page numbers when referring to specific parts of your source:

1 Cor. 13:1 (Revised Standard Version)

Specific Parts of a Source

To cite a specific part of a source, indicate the page, chapter, figure, table, or equation at the appropriate point in text. Always give page numbers for quotations (see Quotation of Sources, pp. 125–126). Note that the words *page* and *chapter* are abbreviated in such text citations:

(Cheek & Buss, 1981, p. 332)

(Shimamura, 1989, chap. 3)

For electronic sources that do not provide page numbers, use the paragraph number, if available, preceded by the ¶ symbol or the abbreviation para. If neither paragraph nor page numbers are visible, cite the heading and the number of the paragraph following it to direct the reader to the location of the material (see Citation of Sources, pp. 128–129).

(Myers, 2000, ¶ 5)

(Beutler, 2000, Conclusion section, para. 1)

To cite parts of classical works (see Classical Works, p. 135), use the specific line, book, and section numbers as appropriate, and *do not* provide page numbers, even for direct quotations.

Personal Communications

Personal communications may be letters, memos, some electronic communications (e.g., e-mail or messages from nonarchived discussion groups or electronic bulletin boards), personal interviews, telephone conversations, and the like. Because they do not provide recoverable data, personal communications are not included in the reference list. Cite personal communications in text only. Give the initials as well as the surname of the communicator, and provide as exact a date as possible:

T. K. Lutes (personal communication, April 18, 2001)

(V.-G. Nguyen, personal communication, September 28, 1998)

For information on electronic media that may be listed in the References, see section I of chapter 9. Use your judgment in citing other electronic forms as personal communications; computer networks (including the Internet) currently provide a casual forum for communicating, and what you cite should have scholarly relevance.

Citations in Parenthetical Material

In a citation that appears in parenthetical text, use commas (not brackets) to set off the date:

(see Table 2 of Hashtroudi, Chrosniak, & Schwartz, 1991, for complete data)

Reference List

The reference list at the end of a journal article documents the article and provides the information necessary to identify and retrieve each source. Authors should choose references judiciously and must include only the sources that were used in the research and preparation of the article.

References in APA publications are cited in text with an author–date citation system and are listed alphabetically in the References section in APA Style.

References to Legal Materials

Legal periodicals and APA journals differ in the placement and format of references. The main difference is that legal periodicals cite references in footnotes, whereas APA journals locate all references, including references to legal materials, in the reference list. For most references, you should use APA format as described in this chapter. References to legal materials, however, which include court decisions, statutes, and other legislative materials, and various secondary sources, will be more useful to the reader if they provide the information in the conventional format of legal citations. For more information on preparing these and other kinds of legal references consult the latest edition of *The Bluebook: A Uniform System of Citation* (2000) or Appendix D of the fifth edition of the *Publication Manual.*

Construction of an Accurate and Complete Reference List

Because one purpose of listing references is to enable readers to retrieve and use the sources, reference data must be correct and complete. Each entry usually contains the following elements: author, year of publication, title, and publishing data—all the information necessary for unique identification and library search. The best way to ensure that information is accurate and complete is to check each reference carefully against the original publication. Give special attention to spelling of proper names and of words in foreign languages, including accents or other special marks, and to completeness of journal titles, years, volume numbers, and page numbers.

APA Reference Style

Because a reference list includes only references that document the article and provide recoverable data, do not include personal communications, such as letters, memoranda, and informal electronic communication. Instead, cite personal communications only in text (see Personal Communications, pp. 136–137, for format).

Abbreviations. Acceptable abbreviations in the reference list for parts of books and other publications include

chap.	chapter
ed.	edition
Rev. ed.	revised edition
2nd ed.	second edition
Ed. (Eds.)	Editor (Editors)
Trans.	Translator(s)
n.d.	no date
p. (pp.)	page (pages)
Vol.	Volume (as in Vol. 4)
vols.	volumes (as in 4 vols.)
No.	Number
Pt.	Part
Tech. Rep.	Technical Report
Suppl.	Supplement

Publishers' Locations. Give the location (city and state for U.S. publishers, city, state or province if applicable, and country for publishers outside of the United States) of the publishers of books, reports, brochures, and other separate, nonperiodical publications. If the publisher is a university and the name of the state (or province) is included in the name of the university, do not repeat the name in the publisher location. The names of U.S. states and territories are abbreviated in the reference list and in the Method section (suppliers' locations); use the official two-letter U.S. Postal Service abbreviations. The following locations can be listed without a state abbreviation or country because they are major cities that are well known for publishing:

Baltimore	New York	Amsterdam	Paris
Boston	Philadelphia	Jerusalem	Rome
Chicago	San Francisco	London	Stockholm
Los Angeles		Milan	Tokyo
		Moscow	Vienna

Arabic Numerals. Although some volume numbers of books and journals are given in roman numerals, APA journals use arabic numerals (e.g., Vol. 3, not Vol. III) because they use less space and are easier to comprehend than roman numerals. A roman numeral that is part of a title should remain roman (e.g., *Attention and Performance XIII*).

Order of References in the Reference List

Alphabetizing Names. Arrange entries in alphabetical order by the surname of the first author, using the following rules for special cases:

- Alphabetize letter by letter. Remember, however, that "nothing precedes something": Brown, J. R., precedes Browning, A. R., even though *i* precedes *j* in the alphabet.
- Alphabetize the prefixes M', Mc, and Mac literally, not as if they were all spelled *Mac*. Disregard the apostrophe: MacArthur precedes McAllister, and MacNeil precedes M'Carthy.
- Alphabetize surnames that contain articles and prepositions (de, la, du, von, etc.) according to the rules of

the language of origin. If you know that a prefix is commonly part of the surname (e.g., De Vries), treat the prefix as part of the last name and alphabetize by the prefix (e.g., DeBase precedes De Vries). If the prefix is not customarily used (e.g., Helmholtz rather than von Helmholtz), disregard it in the alphabetization and place the prefix following the initials (e.g., Helmholtz, H. L. F. von). The biographical section of *Merriam-Webster's Collegiate Dictionary* is a helpful guide on surnames with articles or prepositions.

- Alphabetize entries with numerals as if the numerals were spelled out.

Order of Several Works by the Same First Author. When ordering several works by the same first author, give the author's name in the first and all subsequent references, and use the following rules to arrange the entries:

- One-author entries by the same author are arranged by year of publication, the earliest first:

  Hewlett, L. S. (1996).

  Hewlett, L. S. (1999).

- One-author entries precede multiple-author entries beginning with the same surname:

  Alleyne, R. L. (2001).

  Alleyne, R. L., & Evans, A. J. (1999).

- References with the same first author and different second or third authors are arranged alphabetically by the surname of the second author or, if the second author is the same, the surname of the third author, and so on:

  Gosling, J. R., Jerald, K., & Belfar, S. F. (2000).

  Gosling, J. R., & Tevlin, D. F. (1996).

  Hayward, D., Firsching, A., & Brown, J. (1999).

  Hayward, D., Firsching, A., & Smigel, J. (1999).

- References with the same authors in the same order are arranged by year of publication, the earliest first:

  Cabading, J. R., & Wright, K. (2000).

  Cabading, J. R., & Wright, K. (2001).

- References by the same author (or by the same two or more authors in the same order) with the same publication date are arranged alphabetically by the title (excluding *A* or *The*) that follows the date.

Exception: If the references with the same authors published in the same year are identified as articles in a series (e.g., Part 1 and Part 2), order the references in the series order, not alphabetically by title.

Lowercase letters—*a, b, c,* and so on—are placed immediately after the year, within the parentheses:

Baheti, J. R. (2001a). Control. . . .

Baheti, J. R. (2001b). Roles of. . . .

Order of Several Works by Different First Authors With the Same Surname. Works by different authors with the same surname are arranged alphabetically by the first initial:

Mathur, A. L., & Wallston, J. (1999).

Mathur, S. E., & Ahlers, R. J. (1998).

Note: Include initials with the surname of the first author in the text citations (see Authors With the Same Surname, p. 134).

Order of Works With Group Authors or With No Authors. Occasionally a work will have as its author an agency, association, or institution, or it will have no author at all.

Alphabetize group authors, such as associations or government agencies, by the first significant word of the name. Full official names should be used (e.g., American Psychological Association, not APA). A parent body precedes a subdivision (e.g., University of Michigan, Department of Psychology).

If, *and only if,* the work is signed "Anonymous," the entry begins with the word *Anonymous* spelled out, and the entry is alphabetized as if Anonymous were a true name.

If there is no author, the title moves to the author position, and the entry is alphabetized by the first significant word of the title.

Treat legal references like references with no author; that is, alphabetize legal references by the first significant item in the entry (word or abbreviation).

References Included in a Meta-Analysis

To conserve journal pages, do not list the studies included in a meta-analysis in a separate appendix. Instead, integrate these studies alphabetically within the References section, and identify each by preceding it with an asterisk.

Bandura, A. J. (1977). *Social learning theory.* Englewood Cliffs, NJ: Prentice Hall.

*Bretschneider, J. G., & McCoy, N. L. (1968). Sexual interest and behavior in healthy 80- to 102-year-olds. *Archives of Sexual Behavior, 14,* 343–350.

Add the following statement before the first reference entry: References marked with an asterisk indicate studies included in the meta-analysis. The in-text citations to studies selected for meta-analysis are not preceded by asterisks.

Introduction to APA Reference Style

The next sections describe the main elements of the most common types of references in the order in which they would appear in an entry. Detailed notes on style and punctuation accompany the description of each element, and example numbers given in parentheses correspond to examples in chapter 9.

General Forms

Periodical:

Author, A. A., Author, B. B., & Author, C. C. (1994). Title of article. *Title of Periodical, xx,* xxx–xxx.

Periodicals include items published on a regular basis: journals, magazines, scholarly newsletters, and so on.

Nonperiodical:

Author, A. A. (1994). *Title of work.* Location: Publisher.

Part of a nonperiodical (e.g., book chapter):

Author, A. A., & Author, B. B. (1994). Title of chapter. In A. Editor, B. Editor, & C. Editor (Eds.), *Title of book* (pp. xxx–xxx). Location: Publisher.

Nonperiodicals include items published separately: books, reports, brochures, certain monographs, manuals, and audiovisual media.

Online periodical:

Author, A. A., Author, B. B., & Author, C. C. (2000). Title of article. *Title of Periodical, xx*, xxx–xxx. Retrieved month day, year, from source.

Online document:

Author, A. A. (2000). *Title of work.* Retrieved month day, year, from source.

Electronic sources include aggregated databases, online journals, Web sites or Web pages, newsgroups, Web- or e-mail-based discussion groups, and Web- or e-mail-based newsletters.

Authors

Periodical:

Kernis, M. H., Cornell, D. P., Sun, C.-R., Berry, A., & Harlow, T. (1993). There's more to self-esteem than whether it is high or low: The importance of stability of self-esteem. *Journal of Personality and Social Psychology, 65*, 1190–1204.

Nonperiodical:

Robinson, D. N. (Ed.). (1992). *Social discourse and moral judgment.* San Diego, CA: Academic Press.

- Invert all authors' names; give surnames and initials for only up to and including seven authors. When authors number eight or more, abbreviate the seventh and subsequent authors as et al. [not italicized and with a period after "al"]. In text, follow the citation guidelines in One Work by Multiple Authors, pp. 132–133.
- If an author's first name is hyphenated, retain the hyphen and include a period after each initial.
- Use commas to separate authors, to separate surnames and initials, and to separate initials and suffixes (e.g., Jr. and III); with two or more authors, use an ampersand (&) before the last author.
- Spell out the full name of a group author (e.g., Australian In Vitro Fertilization Collaborative Group; National Institute of Mental Health).
- If authors are listed with the word *with,* include them in the reference in parentheses, for example,

Bulatao, E. (with Winford, C. A.). The text citation, however, refers to the primary author only.

- In a reference to an edited book, place the editors' names in the author position, and enclose the abbreviation Ed. or Eds. in parentheses after the last editor's name.
- In a reference to a work with no author, move the title to the author position, before the date of publication (see chap. 9, Example 26).
- Finish the element with a period. In a reference to a work with a group author (e.g., study group, government agency, association, corporation), the period follows the author element. In a reference to an edited book, the period follows the parenthetical abbreviation (Eds.). In a reference to a work with no author, the period follows the title, which is moved to the author position. (When an author's initial with a period ends the element, do not add an extra period.)

Publication Date

Fowers, B. J., & Olson, D. H. **(1993).** ENRICH Marital Satisfaction Scale: A brief research and clinical tool. *Journal of Family Psychology, 7,* 176–185. [journals, books, audiovisual media]

(1993, June). [meetings; monthly magazines, newsletters, and newspapers]

(1994, September 28). [dailies and weeklies]

(in press). [any work accepted for publication but not yet printed]

(n.d.). [work with no date available]

- Give in parentheses the year the work was copyrighted (for unpublished works, give the year the work was produced).
- For magazines, newsletters, and newspapers, give the year followed by the exact date on the publication (month or month and day; see chap. 9, Examples 6–11), in parentheses.
- Write in press in parentheses for articles that have been accepted for publication but that have not yet

been published. Do not give a date until the article has actually been published. (To reference a paper that is still in revision and under review, see chap. 9, Example 60. See Examples 58–61 for references to unpublished manuscripts.)

- For papers and posters presented at meetings, give the year and month of the meeting, separated by a comma and enclosed in parentheses.
- If no date is available, write n.d. in parentheses.
- Finish the element with a period after the closing parenthesis.

Title of Article or Chapter

Periodical:

Deutsch, F. M., Lussier, J. B., & Servis, L. J. (1993). **Husbands at home: Predictors of paternal participation in childcare and housework.** *Journal of Personality and Social Psychology, 65*, 1154–1166.

Nonperiodical:

O'Neil, J. M., & Egan, J. (1992). **Men's and women's gender role journeys: Metaphor for healing, transition, and transformation.** In B. R. Wainrib (Ed.), *Gender issues across the life cycle* (pp. 107–123). New York: Springer.

- Capitalize only the first word of the title and of the subtitle, if any, and any proper nouns; do not italicize the title or place quotation marks around it.
- Enclose nonroutine information that is important for identification and retrieval in brackets immediately after the article title. Brackets indicate a description of form, not a title. Following are some of the more common notations that help identify works.

Notation	Example
[Letter to the editor]	11
[Special issue]	12
[Monograph]	15
[Abstract]	16

- Finish the element with a period.

Title of Work and Publication Information: Periodicals

Journal:

Buss, D. M., & Schmitt, D. P. (1993). Sexual strategies theory: An evolutionary perspective on human mating. ***Psychological Review, 100,*** **204–232.**

Magazine:

Henry, W. A., III. (1990, April 9). Beyond the melting pot. ***Time, 135,*** **28–31.**

- Give the periodical title in full, in uppercase and lowercase letters.
- Give the volume number of journals, magazines, and newsletters. Do not use Vol. before the number. If, and only if, each issue of a journal begins on page 1, give the issue number in parentheses immediately after the volume number (see chap. 9, Example 2).
- If a journal or newsletter does not use volume numbers, include the month, season, or other designation with the year, for example (1994, April).
- Italicize the name of the periodical and the volume number, if any.
- Give inclusive page numbers. Use pp. before the page numbers in references to newspapers. (Note that in electronic sources, page numbers are often not relevant—see chap. 9, Examples 72–74).
- Use commas after the title and volume number.
- Finish the element with a period.

Title of Work: Nonperiodicals

Saxe, G. B. (1991). **Cultural and cognitive development: Studies in mathematical understanding.** Hillsdale, NJ: Erlbaum.

- Capitalize only the first word of the title and of the subtitle, if any, and any proper nouns; italicize the title.
- Enclose additional information given on the publication for its identification and retrieval (e.g., edition, report number, volume number) in parentheses immediately after the title. Do not use a period

between the title and the parenthetical information; do not italicize the parenthetical information.

- Enclose a description of the form of the work in brackets (after any parenthetical information) if the information is necessary for identification and retrieval; some examples follow.

Notation	Example
[Brochure]	33
[Motion picture]	65
[Videotape]	65
[CD]	69
[Computer software]	92
[Data file]	94, 95

- If a volume is part of a larger, separately titled series or collection, treat the series and volume titles as a two-part title (see chap. 9, Example 35).
- Finish the element with a period.

Title of Work: Part of a Nonperiodical (Book Chapters)

The title element for an edited book consists of (a) the name of the editor (if any) preceded by the word In and (b) the book title with parenthetical information.

Editor:

Baker, F. M., & Lightfoot, O. B. (1993). Psychiatric care of ethnic elders. **In A. C. Gaw (Ed.),** *Culture, ethnicity, and mental illness* (pp. 517–552). Washington, DC: American Psychiatric Press.

- Because the editor's name is not in the author position, do not invert the name; use initials and surname. Give initials and surnames for *all* editors (for substantial reference works with a large editorial board, naming the lead editor followed by et al. is acceptable).
- With two names, use an ampersand (&) before the second surname, and do not use commas to separate the names. With three or more names, use an ampersand before the final surname, and use commas to separate the names.

- Identify the editor by the abbreviation Ed. in parentheses after the surname.
- For a book with no editor, simply include the word In before the book title.
- Finish this part of the element with a comma.

Book title with parenthetical information:

Baker, F. M., & Lightfoot, O. B. (1993). Psychiatric care of ethnic elders. In A. C. Gaw (Ed.), ***Culture, ethnicity, and mental illness*** **(pp. 517–552).** Washington, DC: American Psychiatric Press.

- Give inclusive page numbers of the article or chapter in parentheses after the title. (Note that in electronic sources, page numbers may not be relevant—see chap. 9, Example 76).
- If additional information is necessary for retrieval (e.g., edition, report number, or volume number), this information precedes the page numbers within the parentheses and is followed by a comma (see chap. 9, Example 36).
- Finish the element with a period.

Publication Information: Nonperiodicals

Location, ST: Publisher.	**Hillsdale, NJ: Erlbaum.**
Location, Province, Country: Publisher.	**Toronto, Ontario, Canada: University of Toronto Press.**
Location, Country: Publisher.	**Oxford, England: Basil Blackwell.**
Major City: Publisher.	**Amsterdam: Elsevier.**

- Give the city and, if the city is not well known for publishing (see APA Reference Style, p. 138) or could be confused with another location, the state or province (and/or country) where the publisher is located as noted on the title page of the book. Use a colon after the location.
- If the publisher is a university and the name of the state or province is included in the name of the uni-

versity, do not repeat the state or province in the publisher location.

- Give the name of the publisher in as brief a form as is intelligible. Write out the names of associations, corporations, and university presses, but omit superfluous terms, such as *Publishers*, *Co.*, or *Inc.*, which are not required to identify the publisher. Retain the words *Books* and *Press*.
- If two or more publisher locations are given, give the location listed first in the book or, if specified, the location of the publisher's home office.
- Finish the element with a period.

Retrieval Information: Electronic Sources

The retrieval statement provides the date the information was retrieved, along with the name and, in some cases, address of the source.

Electronic reference formats recommended by the American Psychological Association. (2000, October 12). **Retrieved October 23, 2000, from http://www.apa.org/journals/webref.html**

Eid, M., & Langeheine, R. (1999). The measurement of consistency and occasion specificity with latent class models: A new model and its application to the measurement of affect. *Psychological Methods, 4,* 100–116. **Retrieved November 19, 2000, from the PsycARTICLES database.**

- If information is obtained from a document on the Internet, provide the Internet address for the document at the end of the retrieval statement.
- If information is retrieved from an aggregated database, providing the name of the database is sufficient; no address is needed.
- Use available from to indicate that the URL leads to information on how to obtain the cited material, rather than to the material itself (see chap. 9, Example 95).
- Finish the retrieval element with a period, *unless* it ends with an Internet address.

9 Reference Examples

This chapter contains examples of references in APA Style. The examples are grouped into the following categories: periodicals; books, brochures, and book chapters; technical and research reports; proceedings of meetings and symposia; doctoral dissertations and master's theses; unpublished works and publications of limited circulation; reviews; audiovisual media; and electronic media.

An index of reference examples precedes the examples in this section. The numbers after each index entry refer to the numbered examples in this section.

How to Proceed if a Reference Example You Need is Not in This Section. The most common kinds of references are illustrated herein. Occasionally, however, you may need to use a reference for a source for which this section does not provide a specific example. In such a case, look over the general forms in the Introduction to APA Reference Style (pp. 142–143) and the examples throughout this chapter; choose the example that is most like your source, and follow that format. When in doubt, provide more information rather than less.

Periodicals

Books, Brochures, and Book Chapters

Technical and Research Reports

Proceedings of Meetings and Symposia

Doctoral Dissertations and Master's Theses

Unpublished Work and Publications of Limited Circulation

Reviews

Audiovisual Media

Electronic Media

Elements of a Reference

Author Variations

Title Variations

Publication Information Variations

Periodicals

Elements of a Reference to a Periodical

Herman, L. M., Kuczaj, S. A., III, & Holder, M. D. (1993). Responses to anomalous gestural sequences by a language-trained dolphin: Evidence for processing of semantic relations and syntactic information. *Journal of Experimental Psychology: General, 122,* 184–194.

Note: For treatment of electronic periodicals, see section I.

Article authors: Herman, L. M., Kuczaj, S. A., III, & Holder, M. D.

Date of publication: (1993).

Article title: Responses to anomalous gestural sequences by a language-trained dolphin: Evidence for processing of semantic relations and syntactic information.

Periodical title and publication information: *Journal of Experimental Psychology: General, 122,* 184–194.

Examples of References to Periodicals

1. Journal article, one author

Mellers, B. A. (2000). Choice and the relative pleasure of consequences. *Psychological Bulletin, 126,* 910–924.

2. Journal article, two authors, journal paginated by issue

Klimoski, R., & Palmer, S. (1993). The ADA and the hiring process in organizations. *Consulting Psychology Journal: Practice and Research, 45*(2), 10–36.

3. Journal article, three to seven authors

Saywitz, K. J., Mannarino, A. P., Berliner, L., & Cohen, J. A. (2000). Treatment for sexually abused children and adolescents. *American Psychologist, 55,* 1040–1049.

4. Journal article, more than seven authors

Wolchik, S. A., West, S. G., Sandler, I. N., Tein, J., Coatsworth, D., Lengua, L., et al. (2000). An experimental evaluation of theory-based mother and mother–child programs for children of divorce. *Journal of Consulting and Clinical Psychology, 68,* 843–856.

- After the sixth author's name and initial, use et al. to indicate the remaining authors of the article.
- In text, use the following parenthetical citation for six or more authors each time (including the first) the work is cited: (Wolchik et al., 2000).

5. Journal article in press

Zuckerman, M., & Kieffer, S. C. (in press). Race differences in face-ism: Does facial prominence imply dominance? *Journal of Personality and Social Psychology.*

- A paper that has been submitted to a journal and accepted for publication is considered in press. (If the paper is still undergoing revision and review, use Example 60 for the appropriate reference format.)
- Do not give a year, a volume, or page numbers until the article is published. In text, use the following parenthetical citation: (Zuckerman & Kieffer, in press).
- If another reference by the same author (or same order of authors for multiple authors) is

included in the list of references, place the in-press entry after the published entry. If there is more than one in-press reference, list the entries alphabetically by the first word after the date element, and assign lowercase letter suffixes to the date element (e.g., in press-a).

6. **Magazine article**

Kandel, E. R., & Squire, L. R. (2000, November 10). Neuroscience: Breaking down scientific barriers to the study of brain and mind. *Science, 290,* 1113–1120.

- Give the date shown on the publication—month for monthlies or month and day for weeklies.
- Give the volume number.

7. **Newsletter article**

Brown, L. S. (1993, Spring). Antidomination training as a central component of diversity in clinical psychology education. *The Clinical Psychologist, 46,* 83–87.

- Give the date as it appears on the issue.
- Give the volume number.

8. **Newsletter article, no author**

The new health-care lexicon. (1993, August/September). *Copy Editor, 4,* 1–2.

- Alphabetize works with no author by the first significant word in the title (in this case, new).
- In text, use a short title (or the full title if it is short) for the parenthetical citation: ("The New Health-Care Lexicon," 1993).
- Give the volume number.

9. **Daily newspaper article, no author**

New drug appears to sharply cut risk of death from heart failure. (1993, July 15). *The Washington Post,* p. A12.

- Alphabetize works with no author by the first significant word in the title.
- In text, use a short title for the parenthetical citation: ("New Drug," 1993).
- Precede page numbers for newspaper articles with p. or pp.

10. Daily newspaper article, discontinuous pages

Schwartz, J. (1993, September 30). Obesity affects economic, social status. *The Washington Post*, pp. A1, A4.

- If an article appears on discontinuous pages, give all page numbers, and separate the numbers with a comma (e.g., pp. B1, B3, B5–B7).

11. Weekly newspaper article, letter to the editor

Berkowitz, A. D. (2000, November 24). How to tackle the problem of student drinking [Letter to the editor]. *The Chronicle of Higher Education*, p. B20.

12. Entire issue or special section of a journal

Barlow, D. H. (Ed.). (1991). Diagnoses, dimensions, and *DSM–IV*: The science of classification [Special issue]. *Journal of Abnormal Psychology, 100*(3).

- To cite an entire issue or special section of a journal (in this example, a special issue), give the editors of the issue and the title of the issue.
- If the issue has no editors, move the issue title to the author position, before the year of publication, and end the title with a period. Alphabetize the reference entry by the first significant word in the title. In text, use a short title for the parenthetical citation, for example: ("Diagnoses," 1991).
- For retrievability, provide the issue number for special issues but the page range for special sections.
- To reference an article within a special issue, simply follow the format shown in Examples 1–4.

13. Monograph with issue number and serial (or whole) number

Harris, P. L., & Kavanaugh, R. D. (1993). Young children's understanding of pretense. *Monographs of the Society for Research in Child Development, 58*(1, Serial No. 231).

- Give the volume number and, immediately after in parentheses, the issue and serial (or whole) numbers. Use Whole instead of Serial if the monograph is identified by a whole number.
- For a monograph that is treated as a separate nonperiodical, see Example 47.

14. Monograph bound separately as a supplement to a journal

Battig, W. F., & Montague, W. E. (1969). Category norms for verbal items in 56 categories: A replication and extension of the Connecticut category norms. *Journal of Experimental Psychology Monographs, 80*(3, Pt. 2).

- Give the issue number and supplement or part number in parentheses immediately after the volume number.

15. Monograph bound into journal with continuous pagination

Ganster, D. C., Schaubroeck, J., Sime, W. E., & Mayes, B. T. (1991). The nomological validity of the Type A personality among employed adults [Monograph]. *Journal of Applied Psychology, 76,* 143–168.

- Include Monograph in brackets as a description of form.

16. Abstract as original source

Woolf, N. J., Young, S. L., Fanselow, M. S., & Butcher, L. L. (1991). MAP-2 expression in cholinoceptive pyramidal cells of rodent cortex and hippocampus is altered by Pavlovian conditioning [Abstract]. *Society for Neuroscience Abstracts, 17,* 480.

- Place the description Abstract in brackets between the abstract title and the period.

17. Abstract from a secondary source (print periodical)

Nakazato, K., Shimonaka, Y., & Homma, A. (1992). Cognitive functions of centenarians: The Tokyo Metropolitan Centenarian Study. *Japanese Journal of Developmental Psychology, 3,* 9–16. Abstract obtained from *PsycSCAN: Neuropsychology*, 1993, *2,* Abstract No. 604.

- The term *secondary source* refers to such things as abstracts, article summaries, book reviews, and so forth. These are derived from *primary sources* (journal articles, books), often by someone other than the original author(s). In scholarly research, it is preferable to read and cite primary sources whenever possible.

18. Journal supplement

Regier, A. A., Narrow, W. E., & Rae, D. S. (1990). The epidemiology of anxiety disorders: The epidemiologic catchment area (ECA) experience. *Journal of Psychiatric Research, 24*(Suppl. 2), 3–14.

- Give the supplement number in parentheses immediately after the volume number.

19. Periodical published annually

Fiske, S. T. (1993). Social cognition and social perception. *Annual Review of Psychology, 44,* 155–194.

- Treat series that have regular publication dates and titles as periodicals, not books. If the subtitle changes in series published regularly, such as topics of published symposia (e.g., the *Nebraska Symposium on Motivation* and the *Annals of the New York Academy of Sciences*), treat the series as a book or chapter in an edited book (see Examples 49 and 50).

20. Non-English journal article, title translated into English

Ising, M. (2000). Intensitätsabhängigkeit evozierter Potenzial im EEG: Sind impulsive Personen Augmenter oder Reducer? [Intensity dependence in event-related EEG potentials: Are impulsive individuals augmenters or reducers?]. *Zeitschrift für Differentielle und Diagnostische Psychologie, 21,* 208–217.

- If the original version of a non-English article is used as the source, cite the original version. Give the original title and, in brackets, the English translation.
- Use diacritical marks and capital letters for non-English words as done in the original language (umlauts and capitals for the nouns in this example).

21. English translation of a journal article, journal paginated by issue

Stutte, H. (1972). Transcultural child psychiatry. *Acta Paedopsychiatrica, 38*(9), 229–231.

- If the English translation of a non-English article is used as the source, cite the English translation. Give the English title without brackets (for use of brackets with non-English works, see Examples 20, 31, and 37).

22. Citation of a work discussed in a secondary source

- Give the secondary source in the reference list; in text, name the original work, and give a citation for the secondary source. For example, if Seidenberg and McClelland's work is cited in Coltheart et al. and you did not read the work cited, list the Coltheart et al. reference in the References. In the text, use the following citation:

Text citation:

Seidenberg and McClelland's study (as cited in Coltheart, Curtis, Atkins, & Haller, 1993)

Reference list entry:

Coltheart, M., Curtis, B., Atkins, P., & Haller, M. (1993). Models of reading aloud: Dual-route and parallel-distributed-processing approaches. *Psychological Review, 100,* 589–608.

Books, Brochures, and Book Chapters

Elements of a Reference to an Entire Book

Beck, C. A. J., & Sales, B. D. (2001). *Family mediation: Facts, myths, and future prospects.* Washington, DC: American Psychological Association.

Book authors or editors: Beck, C. A. J., & Sales, B. D.

Date of publication: (2001).

Book title: *Family mediation: Facts, myths, and future prospects.*

Publication information: Washington, DC: American Psychological Association.

- If a book has more than six authors, follow the rule for journals (see Example 4) and abbreviate remaining authors as et al. [not italicized and with a period after "al"] in the first and subsequent text citations. However, because et al. translates to "and others," a decision was made to spell out six authors and seven authors and to use et al. after the sixth author for eight or more authors.

Examples of References to Entire Books

23. Book, third edition, Jr. in name

Mitchell, T. R., & Larson, J. R., Jr. (1987). *People in organizations: An introduction to organizational behavior* (3rd ed.). New York: McGraw-Hill.

24. Book, group author (government agency) as publisher

Australian Bureau of Statistics. (1991). *Estimated resident population by age and sex in statistical local areas, New South Wales, June 1990* (No. 3209.1). Canberra, Australian Capital Territory: Author.

- Alphabetize group authors by the first significant word of the name.
- When the author and publisher are identical, use the word Author as the name of the publisher.

25. Edited book

Gibbs, J. T., & Huang, L. N. (Eds.). (1991). *Children of color: Psychological interventions with minority youth.* San Francisco: Jossey-Bass.

- *Note.* For a book with just one author and an editor as well, list the editor in parentheses after the title, as a translator is treated (see Example 32).

26. Book, no author or editor

Merriam-Webster's collegiate dictionary (10th ed.). (1993). Springfield, MA: Merriam-Webster.

- Place the title in the author position.
- Alphabetize books with no author or editor by the first significant word in the title (Merriam in this case).
- In text, use a few words of the title, or the whole title if it is short, in place of an author name in the citation: (Merriam-Webster's Collegiate Dictionary, 1993).

27. Book, revised edition

Rosenthal, R. (1987). *Meta-analytic procedures for social research* (Rev. ed.). Newbury Park, CA: Sage.

28. Several volumes in a multivolume edited work, publication over period of more than 1 year

Koch, S. (Ed.). (1959–1963). *Psychology: A study of science* (Vols. 1–6). New York: McGraw-Hill.

- In text, use the following parenthetical citation: (Koch, 1959–1963).

29. *Diagnostic and Statistical Manual of Mental Disorders*

American Psychiatric Association. (1994). *Diagnostic and statistical manual of mental disorders* (4th ed.). Washington, DC: Author.

- The association is both author and publisher.
- Cite the edition you used, with arabic numerals, in parentheses.
- In text, cite the name of the association and the name of the manual in full at the first mention in the text; thereafter, you may refer to the traditional *DSM* form (italicized) as follows:

DSM–III	(1980)	third edition
DSM–III–R	(1987)	third edition, revised
DSM–IV	(1994)	fourth edition
DSM–IV–TR	(2000)	text revision

30. Encyclopedia or dictionary

Sadie, S. (Ed.). (1980). *The new Grove dictionary of music and musicians* (6th ed., Vols. 1–20). London: Macmillan.

- For major reference works with a large editorial board, you may list the name of the lead editor, followed by et al.

31. Non-English book

Piaget, J., & Inhelder, B. (1951). *La genèse de l'idée de hasard chez l'enfant* [The origin of the idea of chance in the child]. Paris: Presses Universitaires de France.

- If the original version of a non-English book is used as the source, cite the original version: Give the original title and, in brackets, the English translation.

32. English translation of a book

Laplace, P.-S. (1951). *A philosophical essay on probabilities* (F. W. Truscott & F. L. Emory, Trans.). New York: Dover. (Original work published 1814)

- If the English translation of a non-English work is used as the source, cite the English translation: Give the English title without brackets (for use of brackets with non-English works, see Examples 20, 31, and 37).

- In text, cite the original publication date and the date of the translation: (Laplace, 1814/1951).

33. Brochure, corporate author

Research and Training Center on Independent Living. (1993). *Guidelines for reporting and writing about people with disabilities* (4th ed.) [Brochure]. Lawrence, KS: Author.

- Format references to brochures in the same way as those to entire books.
- In brackets, identify the publication as a brochure.

Elements of a Reference to an Article or Chapter in an Edited Book

Massaro, D. (1992). Broadening the domain of the fuzzy logical model of perception. In H. L. Pick Jr., P. van den Broek, & D. C. Knill (Eds.), *Cognition: Conceptual and methodological issues* (pp. 51–84). Washington, DC: American Psychological Association.

Article or chapter author: Massaro, D.

Date of publication: (1992).

Article or chapter title: Broadening the domain of the fuzzy logical model of perception.

Book editors: In H. L. Pick Jr., P. van den Broek, & D. C. Knill (Eds.),

Book title and article or chapter page numbers: *Cognition: Conceptual and methodological issues* (pp. 51–84).

Publication information: Washington, DC: American Psychological Association.

Examples of References to Articles or Chapters in Edited Books

34. Article or chapter in an edited book, two editors

Bjork, R. A. (1989). Retrieval inhibition as an adaptive mechanism in human memory. In H. L. Roediger III & F. I. M. Craik (Eds.), *Varieties of memory & consciousness* (pp. 309–330). Hillsdale, NJ: Erlbaum.

- For a chapter in a book that is not edited, include the word In before the book title.

35. Article or chapter in an edited book in press, separately titled volume in a multivolume work (two-part title)

Auerbach, J. S. (in press). The origins of narcissism and narcissistic personality disorder: A theoretical and empirical reformulation. In J. M. Masling & R. F. Bornstein (Eds.), *Empirical studies of psychoanalytic theories: Vol. 4. Psychoanalytic perspectives on psychopathology.* Washington, DC: American Psychological Association.

- Do not give the year unless the book is published. In text, use the following parenthetical citation: (Auerbach, in press).
- Page numbers are not available until a work is published; therefore, you cannot give inclusive page numbers for articles or chapters in books that are in press.

36. Chapter in a volume in a series

Maccoby, E. E., & Martin, J. (1983). Socialization in the context of the family: Parent–child interaction. In P. H. Mussen (Series Ed.) & E. M. Hetherington (Vol. Ed.), *Handbook of child psychology: Vol. 4. Socialization, personality, and social development* (4th ed., pp. 1–101). New York: Wiley.

- List the series editor first and the volume editor second so that they will be parallel with the titles of the works.

37. Non-English article or chapter in an edited book, title translated into English

Davydov, V. V. (1972). De introductie van het begrip grootheid in de eerste klas van de basisschool: Een experimenteel onderzoek [The introduction of the concept of quantity in the first grade of the primary school: An experimental study]. In C. F. Van Parreren & J. A. M. Carpay (Eds.), *Sovjetpsychologen aan het woord* (pp. 227–289). Groningen, the Netherlands: Wolters-Noordhoff.

- If the original version of a non-English article or chapter is used as the source, cite the original version: Give the original title and, in brackets, the English translation.

38. Entry in an encyclopedia

Bergmann, P. G. (1993). Relativity. In *The new encyclopaedia Britannica* (Vol. 26, pp. 501–508). Chicago: Encyclopaedia Britannica.

- If an entry has no byline, place the title in the author position.

39. **English translation of an article or chapter in an edited book, volume in a multivolume work, republished work**

Freud, S. (1961). The ego and the id. In J. Strachey (Ed. & Trans.), *The standard edition of the complete psychological works of Sigmund Freud* (Vol. 19, pp. 3–66). London: Hogarth Press. (Original work published 1923)

- If the English translation of a non-English work is used as the source, cite the English translation: Give the English title without brackets (for use of brackets with non-English works, see Examples 20, 31, and 37).
- To identify a translator, use Trans., and place the translator's name after the editor's name. When the editor is also the translator, identify both roles in parentheses after the editor's name.
- In text, use the following parenthetical citation: (Freud, 1923/1961).

40. **English translation of an article or chapter in an edited book, reprint from another source**

Piaget, J. (1988). Extracts from Piaget's theory (G. Gellerier & J. Langer, Trans.). In K. Richardson & S. Sheldon (Eds.), *Cognitive development to adolescence: A reader* (pp. 3–18). Hillsdale, NJ: Erlbaum. (Reprinted from *Manual of child psychology*, pp. 703–732, by P. H. Mussen, Ed., 1970, New York: Wiley)

- If the English translation of a non-English work is used as the source, cite the English translation: Give the English title without brackets (for use of brackets with non-English works, see Examples 20, 31, and 37). In text, use the following parenthetical citation: (Piaget, 1970/1988).

Technical and Research Reports

Mazzeo, J., Druesne, B., Raffeld, P. C., Checketts, K. T., & Muhlstein, A. (1991). *Comparability of computer and paper-and-pencil scores for two CLEP general examinations* (College Board Rep. No. 91–5). Princeton, NJ: Educational Testing Service.

Elements of a Reference to a Report

Report authors: Mazzeo, J., Druesne, B., Raffeld, P. C., Checkettts, K. T., & Muhlstein, A.

Date of publication: (1991).

Report title: *Comparability of computer and paper-and-pencil scores for two CLEP general examinations* (College Board Rep. No. 91-5).

- If the issuing organization assigned a number (e.g., report number, contract number, monograph number) to the report, give that number in parentheses immediately after the title. Do not use a period between the report title and the parenthetical material; do not italicize the parenthetical material. If the report carries two numbers, give the number that best aids identification and retrieval.

Publication information: Princeton, NJ: Educational Testing Service.

- Give the name, exactly as it appears on the publication, of the specific department, office, agency, or institute that published or produced the report. Also, give the higher department, office, agency, or institute if the office that produced the report is not well known. For example, if the National Institute on Drug Abuse, an institute of the U.S. Department of Health and Human Services, produced the report, give only the institute as publisher. Because this institute is well known, it is not necessary to give the higher department as well. If you include the higher department, give the higher department first, then the specific department (see Examples 46 and 47).
- For reports from a document deposit service (e.g., NTIS or ERIC), enclose the document number in parentheses at the end of the entry (see Examples 42 and 43). Do not use a period after the document number.

Examples of References to Reports

41. Report available from the Government Printing Office (GPO), government institute as group author

National Institute of Mental Health. (1990). *Clinical training in serious mental illness* (DHHS Publication No. ADM 90-1679). Washington, DC: U.S. Government Printing Office.

- Government documents available from GPO should show GPO as the publisher.

42. Report available from the National Technical Information Service (NTIS)

Osgood, D. W., & Wilson, J. K. (1990). *Covariation of adolescent health problems.* Lincoln: University of Nebraska. (NTIS No. PB 91-154 377/AS)

- Give the NTIS number in parentheses at the end of the entry.

43. Report available from the Educational Resources Information Center (ERIC)

Mead, J. V. (1992). *Looking at old photographs: Investigating the teacher tales that novice teachers bring with them* (Report No. NCRTL-RR-92-4). East Lansing, MI: National Center for Research on Teacher Learning. (ERIC Document Reproduction Service No. ED346082)

- Give the ERIC number in parentheses at the end of the entry.

44. Government report not available from GPO or a document deposit service

U.S. Department of Health and Human Services. (1992). *Pressure ulcers in adults: Prediction and prevention* (AHCPR Publication No. 92-0047). Rockville, MD: Author.

45. Government report not available from GPO or a document deposit service, article or chapter in an edited collection

Matthews, K. A. (1985). Assessment of Type A behavior, anger, and hostility in epidemiologic studies of cardiovascular disease. In A. M. Ostfield & E. D. Eaker (Eds.), *Measuring psychological variables in epidemiologic studies of cardiovascular disease* (NIH Publication No. 85-2270, pp. 153–183). Washington, DC: U.S. Department of Health and Human Services.

- In parentheses immediately after the title of the collection, give the inclusive page numbers of the article or chapter as well as the number of the report.

46. Report from a university

Broadhurst, R. G., & Maller, R. A. (1991). *Sex offending and recidivism* (Tech. Rep. No. 3). Nedlands, Western Australia: University of Western Australia, Crime Research Centre.

- If the name of the state, province, or country is included in the name of the university, do not repeat the state, province, or country in the publisher location.
- Give the name of the university first, then the name of the specific department or organization that produced the report.

47. Report from a university, edited report, monograph

Shuker, R., Openshaw, R., & Soler, J. (Eds.). (1990). *Youth, media, and moral panic in New Zealand: From hooligans to video nasties* (Delta Research Monograph No. 11). Palmerston North, New Zealand: Massey University, Department of Education.

48. Report from a private organization

Employee Benefit Research Institute. (1992, February). *Sources of health insurance and characteristics of the uninsured* (Issue Brief No. 123). Washington, DC: Author.

- Use this form for issue briefs, working papers, and other corporate documents, with the appropriate document number for retrieval in parentheses.

Proceedings of Meetings and Symposia

49. Published proceedings, published contribution to a symposium, article or chapter in an edited book

Deci, E. L., & Ryan, R. M. (1991). A motivational approach to self: Integration in personality. In R. Dienstbier (Ed.), *Nebraska Symposium on Motivation: Vol. 38. Perspectives on motivation* (pp. 237–288). Lincoln: University of Nebraska Press.

- Capitalize the name of the symposium, which is a proper noun.
- If the name of the state, province, or country is included in the name of the university, do not repeat the state, province, or country in the publisher location.

50. Proceedings published regularly

Cynx, J., Williams, H., & Nottebohm, F. (1992). Hemispheric differences in avian song discrimination. *Proceedings of the National Academy of Sciences, USA, 89,* 1372–1375.

- Treat regularly published proceedings as periodicals.

- *Note:* If only an abstract of the article appears in the proceedings, insert [Abstract] after the article title and before the period. Use brackets to show that the material is a description of form, not a title.

51. Unpublished contribution to a symposium

Lichstein, K. L., Johnson, R. S., Womack, T. D., Dean, J. E., & Childers, C. K. (1990, June). Relaxation therapy for polypharmacy use in elderly insomniacs and noninsomniacs. In T. L. Rosenthal (Chair), *Reducing medication in geriatric populations.* Symposium conducted at the meeting of the First International Congress of Behavioral Medicine, Uppsala, Sweden.

- Give the month of the symposium.

52. Unpublished paper presented at a meeting

Lanktree, C., & Briere, J. (1991, January). *Early data on the Trauma Symptom Checklist for Children (TSC-C).* Paper presented at the meeting of the American Professional Society on the Abuse of Children, San Diego, CA.

53. Poster session

Ruby, J., & Fulton, C. (1993, June). *Beyond redlining: Editing software that works.* Poster session presented at the annual meeting of the Society for Scholarly Publishing, Washington, DC.

- Give the month of the meeting.

Doctoral Dissertations and Master's Theses

54. Doctoral dissertation abstracted in *Dissertation Abstracts International (DAI)* and obtained from UMI

Bower, D. L. (1993). Employee assistant programs supervisory referrals: Characteristics of referring and nonreferring supervisors. *Dissertation Abstracts International, 54* (01), 534B. (UMI No. 9315947)

- If the dissertation is obtained from UMI, give the UMI number as well as the volume and page numbers of *DAI* (see Example 56 for an unpublished doctoral dissertation).
- Prior to Volume 30, the title of *DAI* was *Dissertation Abstracts.*
- Beginning with Volume 27, *Dissertation Abstracts* (and then *DAI*) paginates in two

series: *A. The Humanities and Social Sciences* and *B. The Physical Sciences and Engineering.*

- In 1976, a third and independent series (beginning with Volume 1) was added to *DAI*: *C. European Abstracts*. Beginning with Volume 14, the title of the series was changed to *C. Worldwide.*
- For a master's thesis abstracted in *Masters Abstracts International* and obtained from UMI, use the format shown here, and give as publication information the title, volume number, and page number as well as the UMI number (see Example 57 for an unpublished master's thesis).
- Prior to Volume 24, the title of *Masters Abstracts International* was *Masters Abstracts.*

55. Doctoral dissertation abstracted in *DAI* and obtained from the university

Ross, D. F. (1990). Unconscious transference and mistaken identity: When a witness misidentifies a familiar but innocent person from a lineup (Doctoral dissertation, Cornell University, 1990). *Dissertation Abstracts International, 51,* 417.

- If a manuscript copy of the dissertation from the university was used as the source, give the university and year of the dissertation as well as the volume and page numbers of *DAI.*
- For a master's thesis abstracted in *Masters Abstracts International* and obtained from the university, use the format shown here and give as publication information the title, volume number, and page number of *Masters Abstracts International* as well as the university and year of the thesis (see Example 57 for an unpublished master's thesis).

56. Unpublished doctoral dissertation

Wilfley, D. E. (1989). *Interpersonal analyses of bulimia: Normal-weight and obese.* Unpublished doctoral dissertation, University of Missouri, Columbia.

- If a dissertation does not appear in *DAI,* use the format shown here. (For dissertations that appear in *DAI,* see Examples 54 and 55.)

57. Unpublished master's thesis, university outside the United States

Almeida, D. M. (1990). *Fathers' participation in family work: Consequences for fathers' stress and father–child relations.* Unpublished master's thesis, University of Victoria, Victoria, British Columbia, Canada.

- Give the name of the city and, except for the cities listed in APA Reference Style (p. 138), the name of the state. (Do not give the name of the state if it is included in the name of the university.)
- Give the city and, except for the cities listed in APA Reference Style (p. 138), state or province (if applicable) and country of a university outside the United States.

Unpublished Work and Publications of Limited Circulation

58. Unpublished manuscript not submitted for publication

Stinson, C., Milbrath, C., Reidbord, S., & Bucci, W. (1992). *Thematic segmentation of psychotherapy transcripts for convergent analyses.* Unpublished manuscript.

- For an unpublished manuscript with a university cited, see Example 59.

59. Unpublished manuscript with a university cited

Dépret, E. F., & Fiske, S. T. (1993). *Perceiving the powerful: Intriguing individuals versus threatening groups.* Unpublished manuscript, University of Massachusetts at Amherst.

- Give the name of the city and, if the city is not listed in APA Reference Style (p. 138), the name of the state or province. If the university is located outside the United States, identify the country as well. *Exception:* Do not give the name of the state, province, or country if it is included in the name of the university. In this example, both the city and state are included in the name of the university, so neither is repeated.

60. Manuscript in progress or submitted for publication but not yet accepted

McIntosh, D. N. (1993). *Religion as schema, with implications for the relation between religion and coping.* Manuscript submitted for publication.

- Do not give the name of the journal or publisher to which the manuscript has been submitted.
- Treat a manuscript *accepted* for publication but not yet published as an in-press reference (see Examples 5 and 35).
- Use the same format for a draft or work in progress, but substitute the words Manuscript in preparation for the final sentence. Use the year of the draft you read (not "in preparation") in the text citation.
- Give the university if applicable.

61. Unpublished raw data from study, untitled work

Bordi, F., & LeDoux, J. E. (1993). [Auditory response latencies in rat auditory cortex]. Unpublished raw data.

- Do not italicize the topic; use brackets to indicate that the material is a description of content, not a title.

62. Publication of limited circulation

Klombers, N. (Ed.). (1993, Spring). *ADAA Reporter.* (Available from the Anxiety Disorders Association of America, 6000 Executive Boulevard, Suite 513, Rockville, MD 20852)

- For a publication of limited circulation, give in parentheses immediately after the title a name and address from which the publication can be obtained.
- If a publication can be obtained via the Web, a Web address may be given in place of or in addition to a mailing address (see section I for examples of Web addresses).

Reviews

Elements of a Reference to a Review

Mroczek, D. K. (2000). The emerging study of midlife [Review of the book *Life in the middle: Psychological and social development in middle age*]. *Contemporary Psychology: APA Review of Books, 45,* 482–485.

Review author: Mroczek, D. K.

Date of publication: (2000).

Review title: The emerging study of midlife

Medium being reviewed: Review of the book

Work being reviewed: *Life in the middle: Psychological and social development in middle age.*

Periodical title and publication information: *Contemporary Psychology: APA Review of Books, 45,* 482–485.

Examples of References to Reviews

63. Review of a book

Schatz, B. R. (2000, March 3). Learning by text or context? [Review of the book *The social life of information*]. *Science, 290,* 1304.

- If the review is untitled, use the material in brackets as the title; retain the brackets to indicate that the material is a description of form and content, not a title.
- Identify the type of medium being reviewed in brackets (book, motion picture, television program, etc.).

64. Review of a motion picture

Kraus, S. J. (1992). Visions of psychology: A videotext of classic studies [Review of the motion picture *Discovering Psychology*]. *Contemporary Psychology, 37,* 1146–1147.

Audiovisual Media

65. Motion picture

Scorsese, M. (Producer), & Lonergan, K. (Writer/Director). (2000). *You can count on me* [Motion picture]. United States: Paramount Pictures.

Harrison, J. (Producer), & Schmiechen, R. (Director). (1992). *Changing our minds: The story of Evelyn Hooker* [Motion picture]. (Available from Changing Our Minds, Inc., 170 West End Avenue, Suite 25R, New York, NY 10023)

American Psychological Association (Producer). (2000). *Responding therapeutically to patient expressions of sexual attraction: A stimulus training tape* [Motion picture]. (Available from the American Psychological Association, 750 First Street, NE, Washington, DC 20002–4242)

- Give the name and, in parentheses, the function of the originator or primary contributors (the director or the producer, or both).
- Identify the work as a motion picture in brackets immediately after the title.
- Give the motion picture's country of origin (where it was primarily made and released) as well as the name of the movie studio. Note that depending on the film, a movie studio can be represented by different countries. In the example, the primary production and release of *You Can Count on Me* took place in the United States, but Miramax Films's *Il Postino (The Postman)* was primarily made in Italy and released there first, so the country of origin listed for that film would be Italy.
- When a motion picture is of limited circulation, provide the distributor's name and complete address in parentheses at the end of the reference.

66. Television broadcast

Crystal, L. (Executive Producer). (1993, October 11). *The MacNeil/Lehrer news hour* [Television broadcast]. New York and Washington, DC: Public Broadcasting Service.

67. Television series

Miller, R. (Producer). (1989). *The mind* [Television series]. New York: WNET.

68. Single episode from a television series

Hall, B. (Writer), & Bender, J. (Director). (1991). The rules of the game [Television series episode]. In J. Sander (Producer), *I'll fly away.* New York: New York Broadcasting Company.

- In the author position, list scriptwriters first, followed by the director (identify his or her function in parentheses after the name).
- Place the producer of the series in the editor position.

69. Music recording

General form:

Writer, A. (Date of copyright). Title of song [Recorded by artist if different from writer]. On *Title of album* [Medium of recording:

CD, record, cassette, etc.]. Location: Label. (Recording date if different from copyright date)

Recording:

Shocked, M. (1992). Over the waterfall. On *Arkansas traveler* [CD]. New York: PolyGram Music.

Rerecording by artist other than writer:

Goodenough, J. B. (1982). Tails and trotters [Recorded by G. Bok, A. Mayo, & E. Trickett]. On *And so will we yet* [CD]. Sharon, CT: Folk-Legacy Records. (1990)

- In text citations, include side and band or track numbers: "Tails and Trotters" (Goodenough, 1982, track 5).

70. Audio recording

Costa, P. T., Jr. (Speaker). (1988). *Personality, continuity, and changes of adult life* (Cassette Recording No. 207-433-88A-B). Washington, DC: American Psychological Association.

- Give the name and function of the originators or primary contributors (in this example, Costa, who is the speaker).
- Specify the medium in brackets immediately after the title (in this example, cassette recording). Give a number in parentheses for the recording if it is necessary for identification and retrieval. Brackets are used to identify medium. If medium is indicated as part of retrieval ID, brackets are not needed.
- Give the location and name of the distributor (in this example, American Psychological Association).

Electronic Media

Sources on the Internet

The Internet is a worldwide network of interconnected computers. Although there are a number of methods for navigating and sharing information across the Internet, by far the most popular and familiar is the graphical interface of the World Wide Web. The vast majority of Internet sources cited in APA journals are those that are accessed via the Web.

The variety of material available on the Web, and the variety of ways in which it is structured and presented, can present challenges for creating usable and useful references. Regardless of format, however, authors using and citing Internet sources should observe the following two guidelines:

1. Direct readers as closely as possible to the information being cited—whenever possible, reference specific documents rather than home or menu pages.

2. Provide addresses that work.

Documents available via the Internet include articles from periodicals (e.g., newspaper, newsletter, or journal); they may stand on their own (e.g., research paper, government report, online book or brochure); or they may have a quintessentially Web-based format (e.g., Web page, newsgroup).

At a minimum, a reference of an Internet source should provide a document title or description, a date (either the date of publication or update or the date of retrieval), and an address (in Internet terms, a uniform resource locator, or URL). Whenever possible, identify the authors of a document as well.

The URL is the most critical element—if it doesn't work, readers won't be able to find the cited material, and the credibility of your paper or argument will suffer. The most common reason URLs fail is that they are transcribed or typed incorrectly; the second most common reason is that the document they point to has been moved or deleted.

The components of a URL are as follows:

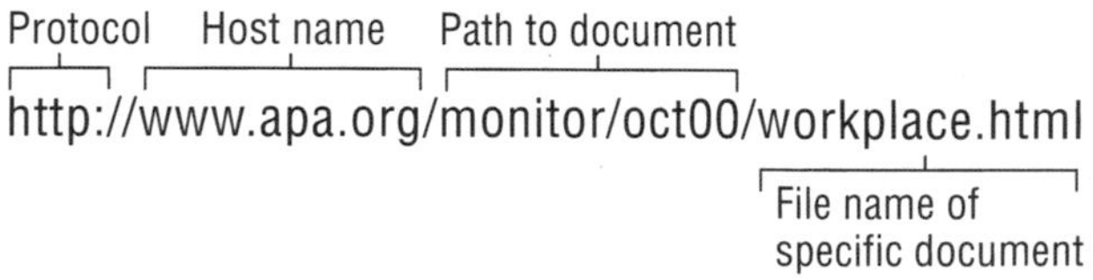

Protocol — Host name — Path to document

http://www.apa.org/monitor/oct00/workplace.html

File name of specific document

The protocol indicates what method a Web browser (or other type of Internet software) should use to exchange data with the file server on which the desired document resides. The protocols recognized by most browsers are hypertext transfer protocol (http), hypertext transfer protocol secure (https), and file transfer protocol (ftp);

other Internet protocols include telnet and gopher. In a URL, all of the protocols listed in this paragraph should be followed by a colon and two forward slashes (e.g., http://).

The host name identifies the server on which the files reside. On the Web, it is often the address for an organization's home page (e.g., http://www.apa.org is the address for APA's home page). Although most host names start with "www," not all do (e.g, http://journals.apa.org is the home page for APA's electronic journals, and http://members.apa.org is the entry page to the members-only portion of the APA site). The host name is not case sensitive; for consistency and ease of reading, always type it in lowercase letters.

The rest of the address indicates the directory path leading to the desired document. This part of the URL is case sensitive; faithfully reproduce uppercase and lowercase letters and all punctuation. It is important to provide the directory path, and not just the host name, because home pages and menu pages typically consist mainly of links, only one of which may be to the document or information you want the readers to find. If there are hundreds of links (or even just 10 to 20), readers may give up in frustration before they have located the material you are citing.

If you are using a word-processing program, the easiest way to transcribe a URL correctly is to copy it directly from the address window in your browser and paste it into your paper (make sure the automatic hyphenation feature of your word processor is turned off). Do not insert a hyphen if you need to break a URL across lines; instead, break the URL after a slash or before a period.

Test the URLs in your references regularly—when you first draft a paper, when you submit it for peer review, when you're preparing the final version for publication, and when you're reviewing the proofs. If the document you are citing has moved, update the URL so that it points to the correct location. If the document is no longer available, you may want to substitute another source (e.g., if you originally cited a draft and a formally published version now exists) or drop it from the paper altogether.

Periodicals on the Internet

71. Internet articles based on a print source

At present, the majority of the articles retrieved from online publications in psychology and the behavioral sciences are exact duplicates of those in their print versions and are unlikely to have additional analyses and data attached. This is likely to change in the future. In the meantime, the same basic primary journal reference (see Examples 1–5) can be used, but if you have viewed the article only in its electronic form, you should add in brackets after the article title [Electronic version] as in the following fictitious example:

VandenBos, G., Knapp, S., & Doe, J. (2001). Role of reference elements in the selection of resources by psychology undergraduates [Electronic version]. *Journal of Bibliographic Research, 5,* 117–123.

If you are referencing an online article that you have reason to believe has been changed (e.g., the format differs from the print version or page numbers are not indicated) or that includes additional data or commentaries, you will need to add the date you retrieved the document and the URL.

VandenBos, G., Knapp, S., & Doe, J. (2001). Role of reference elements in the selection of resources by psychology undergraduates. *Journal of Bibliographic Research, 5,* 117–123. Retrieved October 13, 2001, from http://jbr.org/articles.html

72. Article in an Internet-only journal

Fredrickson, B. L. (2000, March 7). Cultivating positive emotions to optimize health and well-being. *Prevention & Treatment, 3,* Article 0001a. Retrieved November 20, 2000, from http://journals.apa.org/prevention/volume3/pre0030001a.html

73. Article in an Internet-only journal, retrieved via file transfer protocol (ftp)

Crow, T. J. (2000). Did *Homo sapiens* speciate on the *y* chromosome? *Psycoloquy, 11.* Retrieved March 25, 2001, from ftp://ftp.princeton.edu/harnad/Psycoloquy/2000.volume.11/psyc.00.11.001.language-sex-chromosomes.1.crow

74. Article in an Internet-only newsletter

Glueckauf, R. L., Whitton, J., Baxter, J., Kain, J., Vogelgesang, S., Hudson, M., et al. (1998, July). Videocounseling for families of rural teens with epilepsy—Project update. *Telehealth News,*

2(2). Retrieved June 6, 2000, from http://www.telehealth.net/ subscribe/newslettr_4a.html#1

- Use the complete publication date given on the article.
- Note that there are no page numbers.
- In an Internet periodical, volume and issue numbers often are not relevant. If they are not used, the name of the periodical is all that can be provided in the reference.
- Whenever possible, the URL should link directly to the article.
- Break a URL that goes to another line after a slash or before a period. Do not insert (or allow your word-processing program to insert) a hyphen at the break.

Nonperiodical Documents on the Internet

75. Multipage document created by private organization, no date

Greater New Milford (Ct) Area Healthy Community 2000, Task Force on Teen and Adolescent Issues. (n.d.). *Who has time for a family meal? You do!* Retrieved October 5, 2000, from http://www.familymealtime.org

- When an Internet document comprises multiple pages (i.e., different sections have different URLs), provide a URL that links to the home (or entry) page for the document.
- Use n.d. (no date) when a publication date is not available.

76. Chapter or section in an Internet document

Benton Foundation. (1998, July 7). Barriers to closing the gap. In *Losing ground bit by bit: Low-income communities in the information age* (chap. 2). Retrieved August 18, 2001, from http://www.benton.org/Library/Low-Income/two.html

- Use a chapter or section identifier (if available) in place of page numbers.
- Provide a URL that links directly to the chapter or section.

77. Stand-alone document, no author identified, no date

GVU's 8th WWW user survey. (n.d.). Retrieved August 8, 2000, from http://www.cc.gatech.edu/gvu/user_surveys/survey-1997-10/

- If the author of a document is not identified, begin the reference with the title of the document.

78. Document available on university program or department Web site

Chou, L., McClintock, R., Moretti, F., & Nix, D. H. (1993). *Technology and education: New wine in new bottles: Choosing pasts and imagining educational futures.* Retrieved August 24, 2000, from Columbia University, Institute for Learning Technologies Web site: http://www.ilt.columbia.edu/publications/papers/newwine1.html

- If a document is contained within a large and complex Web site (such as that for a university or a government agency), identify the host organization and the relevant program or department before giving the URL for the document itself. Precede the URL with a colon.

Technical and Research Reports on the Internet

79. Report from a university, available on private organization Web site

University of California, San Francisco, Institute for Health and Aging. (1996, November). *Chronic care in America: A 21st century challenge.* Retrieved September 9, 2000, from the Robert Wood Johnson Foundation Web site: http://www.rwjf.org/library/chrcare/

- When the author of a document is markedly different from the provider (e.g., the host organization), explicitly identify the latter in the retrieval statement.
- *Note.* This document is no longer available on this site. In most papers, such a reference should be updated or deleted.

80. U.S. government report available on government agency Web site, no publication date indicated

United States Sentencing Commission. (n.d.). *1997 sourcebook of federal sentencing statistics.* Retrieved December 8, 1999, from http://www.ussc.gov/annrpt/1997/sbtoc97.htm

81. Report from a private organization, available on organization Web site

Canarie, Inc. (1997, September 27). *Towards a Canadian health IWAY: Vision, opportunities and future steps.* Retrieved November 8, 2000, from http://www.canarie.ca/press/publications/pdf/health/healthvision.doc

82. Abstract of a technical report retrieved from university Web site

Kruschke, J. K., & Bradley, A. L. (1995). *Extensions to the delta rule of associative learning* (Indiana University Cognitive Science Research Report No. 14). Abstract retrieved October 21, 2000, from http://www.indiana.edu/~kruschke/deltarule_abstract.html

- If the document retrieved is an abstract rather than a full paper, begin the retrieval statement with Abstract retrieved.

Proceedings of Meetings and Symposia on the Internet

83. Paper presented at a symposium, abstract retrieved from university Web site

Cutler, L. D., Frülich, B., & Hanrahan, P. (1997, January 16). *Two-handed direct manipulation on the responsive workbench.* Paper presented at the 1997 Symposium on Interactive 3D Graphics. Abstract retrieved June 12, 2000, from http://www.graphics.stanford.edu/papers/twohanded/

84. Paper presented at a virtual conference

Tan, G., & Lewandowsky, S. (1996). *A comparison of operator trust in humans versus machines.* Paper presented at the CybErg 96 virtual conference. Retrieved May 16, 2000, from http://www.curtin.edu.au/conference/cyberg/centre/outline.cgi/frame?dir=tan

- Note that there is no geographic location for a virtual conference (i.e., a conference that takes place entirely online).

E-Mail

E-mail sent from one individual to another should be cited as a personal communication (see Personal Communications, pp. 136–137).

Newsgroups, Online Forums and Discussion Groups, and Electronic Mailing Lists

The Internet offers several options for people around the world to sponsor and join discussions devoted to particular subjects. These options include newsgroups, online forums and discussion groups, and electronic mailing lists. (The last are often referred to as "listservs." However, LISTSERV is a trademarked name for a particular software program; "electronic mailing list" is the appropriate generic term.)

Newsgroups can be accessed via Usenet (usually through an e-mail program or news reader); archives of many Usenet newsgroups are also maintained on the Web at http://groups.google.com. Online forums or discussion groups are primarily Web based. Many, but not all, also operate as electronic mailing lists in that messages posted to the forum or discussion are e-mailed to participants.

Care should be taken when citing electronic discussion sources—as a rule, these are not referenced in formal publications because they are generally not peer reviewed, are not regarded as having scholarly content, and are not archived for a significant length of time. Any message or communication you cite should have scholarly value and should be retrievable. Although some newsgroups, online forums and discussion groups, and electronic mailing lists do maintain archives for a limited time, not all do. If no archives are maintained, then the message will not be retrievable and should not be included in the reference list. At best, it can be cited as a personal communication (see Personal Communications, pp. 136–137).

85. Message posted to a newsgroup

Chalmers, D. (2000, November 17). Seeing with sound [Msg 1]. Message posted to news://sci.psychology.consciousness

- If the author's full name is available, list the last name first followed by initials. If only a screen name is available, use the screen name.
- Provide the exact date of the posting.
- Follow the date with the subject line of the message (also referred to as the "thread"); do not italicize it. Provide any identifier for the message in brackets after the title.

- Finish the reference with Message posted to followed by the address of the newsgroup. Note that the protocol is news.

86. Message posted to online forum or discussion group

Simons, D. J. (2000, July 14). New resources for visual cognition [Msg 31]. Message posted to http://groups.yahoo.com/group/visualcognition/message/31

87. Message posted to an electronic mailing list

Hammond, T. (2000, November 20). YAHC: Handle Parameters, DOI Genres, etc. Message posted to Ref-Links electronic mailing list, archived at http://www.doi.org/mail-archive/ref-link/msg00088.html

- Provide the name of the mailing list and the address for the archived version of the message.

Other Electronic Sources

Aggregated Databases. Researchers and students are increasingly making use of aggregated, searchable databases to find and retrieve abstracts, articles, and other types of information. The previous edition of this manual required information about the source and format of the database in addition to information about the material retrieved. These days, however, most databases are available from a variety of sources or suppliers and in a variety of formats (e.g., on CD-ROM, mounted on a university server, available through a supplier Web site). Moreover, the distinctions between these various sources and formats are usually not apparent to the end user.

Therefore, when referencing material obtained by searching an aggregated database, follow the format appropriate to the work retrieved and add a retrieval statement that gives the date of retrieval and the proper name of the database. An item or accession number also may be provided but is not required. If you wish to include this number, put it in parentheses at the end of the retrieval statement.

88. Electronic copy of a journal article, three to five authors, retrieved from database

Borman, W. C., Hanson, M. A., Oppler, S. H., Pulakos, E. D., & White, L. A. (1993). Role of early supervisory experience in supervisor performance. *Journal of Applied Psychology, 78,* 443–449. Retrieved October 23, 2000, from the PsycARTICLES database.

89. Daily newspaper article, electronic version available by search

Hilts, P. J. (1999, February 16). In forecasting their emotions, most people flunk out. *The New York Times.* Retrieved November 21, 2000, from http://www.nytimes.com

90. Electronic copy of an abstract obtained from a secondary database

Fournier, M., de Ridder, D., & Bensing, J. (1999). Optimism and adaptation to multiple sclerosis: What does optimism mean? *Journal of Behavioral Medicine, 22,* 303–326. Abstract retrieved October 23, 2000, from PsycINFO database.

91. Electronic version of U.S. government report available by search from GPO Access database (on the Web)

U.S. General Accounting Office. (1997, February). *Telemedicine: Federal strategy is needed to guide investments* (Publication No. GAO/NSAID/HEHS-97–67). Retrieved September 15, 2000, from General Accounting Office Reports Online via GPO Access: http://www.access.gpo.gov/su_docs/aces/aces160.shtml?/gao/index.html

- The retrieval statement should provide a URL that links directly to the search screen for the database.

Computer Programs, Software, and Programming Languages. Reference entries are not necessary for standard off-the-shelf software and programming languages, such as Microsoft Word, Excel, Java, Adobe Photoshop, and even SAS and SPSS. In text, give the proper name of the software, along with the version number.

Do provide reference entries for specialized software or computer programs with limited distribution.

92. Computer software

Miller, M. E. (1993). The Interactive Tester (Version 4.0) [Computer software]. Westminster, CA: Psytek Services.

93. Computer software and manual available on university Web site

Schwarzer, R. (1989). Statistics software for meta-analysis [Computer software and manual]. Retrieved March 23, 2001, from http://www.yorku.ca/faculty/academic/schwarze/meta_e.htm

- Do not italicize names of software, programs, or languages.
- If an individual has proprietary rights to the software, name him or her as the author; otherwise, treat such references as unauthored works.
- In brackets immediately after the title, identify the source as a computer program, language, or software. Do not use a period between the title and the bracketed material.
- Give the location and the name of the organization that produced the work, if applicable, in the publisher position.
- To reference a manual, give the same information. However, in the brackets after the title, identify the source as a computer program or software manual.

Raw Data

94. Data file, available from government agency

National Health Interview Survey—Current health topics: 1991—Longitudinal study of aging (Version 4) [Data file]. Hyattsville, MD: National Center for Health Statistics.

- In brackets at the end of the title (before the period), give a description of the material (e.g., Data file).

95. Data file, available from NTIS Web site

Department of Health and Human Services, National Center for Health Statistics. (1991). *National Health Provider Inventory: Home health agencies and hospices, 1991* [Data file]. Available from National Technical Information Service Web site, http://www.ntis.gov

- Use Available from to indicate that the URL leads to information on how to obtain the cited material, rather than to the material itself.

References

American Psychological Association. (2001). *Publication manual of the American Psychological Association* (5th ed.). Washington, DC: Author.

American Psychological Association. (2002). Ethical principles of psychologists and code of conduct. *American Psychologist, 57,* 1060–1073.

The bluebook: A uniform system of citation (17th ed.). (2000). Cambridge, MA: Harvard Law Review Association.

Boston, B. O. (1992, November). Portraying people with disabilities: Toward a new vocabulary. *The Editorial Eye, 15,* 1–3, 6–7.

Ehrenberg, A. S. C. (1977). Rudiments of numeracy. *Journal of the Royal Statistical Society A, 140* (Pt. 3), 277–297.

Knatterud, M. E. (1991, February). Writing with the patient in mind: Don't add insult to injury. *American Medical Writers Association Journal, 6,* 10–17.

Maggio, R. (1991). *The bias-free word finder: A dictionary of nondiscriminatory language.* Boston: Beacon Press.

Nicol, A. A. M., & Pexman, P. M. (1999). *Presenting your findings: A practical guide for creating tables.* Washington, DC: American Psychological Association.

Nicol, A. A. M., & Pexman, P. M. (2003). *Displaying your findings: A practical guide for creating figures, posters, and presentations.* Washington, DC: American Psychological Association.

Nurnberg, M. (1972). Punctuation—Who needs it? In *Questions you always wanted to ask about English but were afraid to raise your hand* (pp. 168–241). New York: Washington Square Press.

Pfaffman, C., Young, P. T., Dethier, V. G., Richter, C. P., & Stellar, E. (1954). The preparation of solutions for research in chemoreception and food acceptance. *Journal of Comparative and Physiological Psychology, 47,* 93–96.

Raspberry, W. (1989, January 4). When "Black" becomes "African American." *The Washington Post,* p. A19.

Reisman, S. J. (Ed.). (1962). *A style manual for technical writers and editors.* New York: Macmillan.

Schaie, K. W. (1993). Ageist language in psychological research. *American Psychologist, 48,* 49–51.

Scientific Illustration Committee. (1988). *Illustrating science: Standards for publication.* Bethesda, MD: Council of Biology Editors.

Skillin, M. E., & Gay, R. M. (1974). *Words into type* (3rd ed.). Englewood Cliffs, NJ: Prentice-Hall.

University of Chicago Press. (2003). *The Chicago manual of style* (15th ed.). Chicago: Author.

Wainer, H. (1997). Improving tabular displays: With NAEP tables as examples and inspirations. *Journal of Educational and Behavioral Statistics, 22,* 1–30.

Appendix A
Style Rules Cross-Referenced to the Fifth Edition of the *Publication Manual of the American Psychological Association*

Concise Rules of APA Style section	*Publication Manual* numbered section
1. Concise and Bias-Free Writing	
General Guidance	
Orderly Presentation of Ideas	2.01
Smoothness of Expression	2.02
Economy of Expression	2.03
Precision and Clarity	2.04
Grammar	
Verbs	2.06
Agreement of Subject and Verb	2.07
Pronouns	2.08
Misplaced and Dangling Modifiers and Use of Adverbs	2.09
Relative Pronouns and Subordinate Conjunctions	2.10
Parallel Construction	2.11
Linguistic Devices	2.12
Reducing Bias in Language	
Guideline 1: Describe at the Appropriate Level of Specificity	
Guideline 2: Be Sensitive to Labels	
Guideline 3: Acknowledge Participation	
Gender	2.13

Appendix B
Checklist for Manuscript Submission

Format

- Is the original manuscript printed on 8 ½ × 11 in. (22 × 28 cm) white bond paper?
- Is every component of the manuscript double-spaced?
- Are the margins at least 1 in. (2.54 cm)?
- Are the title page, abstract, references, appendixes, author note, content footnotes, tables, figure captions, and figures on separate pages (with only one table or figure per page)? Are they ordered in sequence, with the text pages between the abstract and the references?
- If the manuscript is to receive masked review, is the author note typed on the title page, which is removed by the journal editor before review?
- Are all pages (except figure pages) numbered in sequence, starting with the title page?

Title Page and Abstract

- Is the title 10 to 12 words?
- Does the byline reflect the institution where the work was conducted?
- Is the abstract no longer than 120 words?

Paragraphs and Headings

- Is each paragraph longer than a single sentence but not longer than one manuscript page?
- Do the levels of headings accurately reflect the organization of the paper?
- Do all headings of the same level appear in the same format?

Abbreviations

- Are any unnecessary abbreviations eliminated and any necessary ones explained?
- Are abbreviations in tables and figures explained in the table notes and figure captions or legends?

Mathematics and Statistics

- Are Greek letters and all but the most common mathematical symbols identified on the manuscript?
- Are all non-Greek letters that are used as statistical symbols for algebraic variables in italics?

Units of Measurement

- Are metric equivalents for all nonmetric units provided?
- Are all metric and nonmetric units with numeric values abbreviated?

References

- Are references cited both in text and in the references list?
- Do the text citations and reference list entries agree both in spelling and in date?
- Are journal titles in the reference list spelled out fully?
- Are the references (both in the parenthetical text citations and in the reference list) ordered alphabetically by the authors' surnames?
- Are inclusive page numbers for all articles or chapters in books provided in the reference list?
- Are references to studies included in your meta-analysis preceded by an asterisk?

Notes and Footnotes

- Is the departmental affiliation given for each author in the author note?
- Does the author note include both the author's current affiliation if it is different from the byline affiliation and a current address for correspondence?
- Does the author note disclose special circumstances about the article (portions presented at a meeting, student paper as basis for the article, report of a longitudinal study, relationship that may be perceived as a conflict of interest)?
- In the text, are all footnotes indicated, and are footnote numbers correctly located?

Tables and Figures

- Does every table column, including the stub column, have a heading?
- Have all vertical table rules been omitted?
- Are the elements in the figures large enough to remain legible after the figure has been reduced to the width of a journal column or page?
- Does lettering in a figure vary by no more than 4 point sizes of type?
- Are glossy or high-quality laser prints of all figures included, and are the prints no larger than 8 ½ × 11 in. (22 × 28 cm)?
- Is each figure labeled with the correct figure number and short article title?
- Are all figures and tables mentioned in the text and numbered in the order in which they are mentioned?

Copyright and Quotations

- Is written permission to use previously published text, tests or portions of tests, tables, or figures enclosed with the manuscript?
- Are page or paragraph numbers provided in text for all quotations?

Submitting the Manuscript

- Have you provided the required number of copies of the manuscript, including the original?
- Are the journal editor's name and address current?
- Is a cover letter included with the manuscript? Does the letter (a) include the author's postal address, e-mail address, telephone number, and fax number for future correspondence and (b) state that the manuscript is original, not previously published, and not under concurrent consideration elsewhere? Does the letter inform the journal editor of the existence of any similar published manuscripts written by the author?

Index